Leadership Through A Screen

Leadership Through A Screen

A Definitive Guide to Leading a Remote, Virtual Team

Dr. Joseph Brady
Dr. Garry Prentice

BEP | BUSINESS EXPERT PRESS

Leadership Through A Screen: A Definitive Guide to Leading a Remote, Virtual Team
Copyright © Business Expert Press, LLC, 2019.

First published in 2019 by
Business Expert Press, LLC
222 East 46th Street, New York, NY 10017
www.businessexpertpress.com

ISBN-13: 978-1-94858-096-0 (paperback)
ISBN-13: 978-1-94858-097-7 (e-book)

Business Expert Press Corporate Communication Collection

Collection ISSN: 2156-8162 (print)
Collection ISSN: 2316-8170 (electronic)

Cover and interior design by S4Carlisle Publishing Services Private Ltd., Chennai, India

First edition: 2019

10 9 8 7 6 5 4 3 2 1

Printed in the United States of America.

Abstract

Leadership Through the Screen is a business leadership guidebook that tells a story. The book defines and helps provide key solutions for some of the greatest leadership challenges facing global managers today. Written in an easy-to-read manner, each chapter highlights a single issue through the eyes of a fictional VP of marketing.

The authors have done the research and included it in these pages so that business leaders do not have to. This book is meant to serve as a map to help modern managers weave their way through many of the fundamental challenges of leading people in a global and virtual realm. It provides the tools, knowledge, and potential solutions these leaders can use to forge successful and productive virtual teams.

Keywords

virtual teams; team trust; technology; psychological contract; remote workers; leadership

Contents

Preface ix

Acknowledgments xi

Chapter 1   Setting the Stage 1

Chapter 2   The Beginning 5

Chapter 3   Technology and the Roles Game 13

Chapter 4   The Rocky Road to Trust 23

Chapter 5   No Time to Lose 31

Chapter 6   Year-End Reviews 37

Chapter 7   The Emotional Game 41

Chapter 8   The Invisible Contract 47

Chapter 9   Filling the Void 61

Chapter 10 What Is Job Satisfaction Anyway? 65

Chapter 11 The Cultural Conundrum 71

Chapter 12 The Lonely, Dark Halls of Isolation 79

Chapter 13 An Additional Perspective 85

Chapter 14 That's a Wrap 91

References 103

About the Authors 119

Index 121

Preface

Make no mistake, leading a virtual team is tough. It is a proverbial minefield of technology, feelings, culture, psychology, and human interaction. Anyone can manage a virtual team, but to do it well, that's another question entirely! While DQ, or digital intelligence, is an important skill to have, it's certainly not everything. To truly *lead* and *inspire* a virtual team, and not just manage a bunch of remote people trying to hit their key performance indicators requires definitive skill, leadership, and personal development. Leadership of a local team certainly has its challenges, but when you throw in virtual communications, geographic separation, and major time differences, managing a team of remotely located human beings can become a frenzied concerto of mixed feelings, confusion, and misinterpretations. People who work remotely in isolation can feel alone, virtual managers can have work/life balance issues and familial pressures due to long hours, and simple verbal or written misunderstandings can have disastrous consequences for the team and possibly even the company. Not only is electronic or e-leadership a challenge, but decision making can be slow, and confusion of job roles can slow the process down. With all of these difficulties, it's no wonder that some say 60 percent of virtual teams fail (Witt 2011).

Taking it even further, in a survey of over 1,000 global, virtual managers in 80 different countries, a whopping 98 percent felt content in their intercultural leadership abilities. However, only 19 percent of virtual team members felt that their team leadership was actually up to the task of leading an intercultural team (Virtual Teams Survey Report 2016)! Is it possible that managers of virtual teams think too highly of their abilities? Are these leaders suffering delusions of grandeur? Or could it simply be that leading a virtual team involves far greater complexity than meets the eye?

The purpose of this book is to simplify the lives of those who are in the position of leading remote, virtual teams. The authors know that remote team leaders don't have a lot of time on their plate. Therefore, we took the time to do the research so busy managers don't have to. To further enhance engagement of the reader with the important topics presented, the book presents a fictional case study of a virtual leader who is trying to adjust to his new role. Through the eyes of this character, we present real, practical, and academic research from multiple sources, including our own study, to streamline the experience and make it visceral and relevant to those who face these challenges on a daily basis. Through the use of this fictional case study, backed up by real research, we provide a practical and useful handbook that can help leaders avoid the inevitable pitfalls that can come with managing people through the technology of computer screens and cell phones.

Acknowledgments

Joseph Brady: I would like to thank my wife, Silvia, for all of her support throughout this project. Thanks to my parents Joe and Joanie for always pushing me to the next level, and to my boys, Alexander and Nicholas, for helping me stay motivated on the writing journey. Thanks to Alexander, especially, who assisted with organization of the bibliography. Thank you to Nigel Wyatt for seeking me out, to Debbie DuFrene for her editing help, and to Rob Zwettler for the opportunity to work with BEP. Furthermore, I thank Christophe Rougeron and Ewan Livesey for their expert management advice on the completed project. Finally, but definitely not least, thanks to Garry. It's been a pleasure working with him in this collaboration, and I thank him for all of his help with this publication.

Garry Prentice: I would like to sincerely thank all the people who provided advice and feedback while writing the book. I dedicate this book to my wife, Nola, my parents, Margaret and Raymond, and my sister, Gail. I also would like to pay special tribute to my writing partner, Joe, whose dedication, enthusiasm, and diligence are inspiring.

CHAPTER 1

Setting the Stage

Hierarchy has dominated human society and culture since the dawn of time. Hierarchal structures often afford those in leadership great power and influence, and in some cases, such as in the military, such otherwise objectionable power may be necessary. However, in other situations, the pursuit of absolute leadership control can lead to potentially disastrous consequences. In business, historic models often necessitated the institutional platform of uninhibited hierarchal levels, leaving little room for those in the lower ranks to challenge given ideas or tasks. Of course, the word *historic* in this context could be considered irrelevant, or even conjectural, when one considers that even today, many companies still follow this traditional method of leadership.

In recent years, however, certain new developments in management have challenged the notion of uninhibited authoritative power. Among these are the proliferation of new leadership models and research, international diversity, the growing trend of employee empowerment, and the diffusion of communication technology. Technology has been the catalyst for new opportunities in both domestic and international business and has provided the opportunity for organizations to expand their search for talent and diversity in markets that were previously beyond their reach.

This global expansion has resulted in novel approaches to how people do business and even in how humans interact in modern society. The continuous development of communications technology has resulted in a shifting paradigm where individuals no longer need to be seated right across one another in an office. Now cross-functional teams can work together, even while members are in different buildings, cities, or continents. Working through electronic communications allows business leadership to manage virtual teams (VTs) that are geographically separate, but still easily accessible. It is quite possible that for some global teams, moving members to corporate headquarters could be quite cost-prohibitive and inefficient. Furthermore, technology has changed the way business people share knowledge, collaborate, and work together and has created a new skill set requirement in the global working landscape (Schwartz, Bersin, and Pelster 2014).

Certainly, there are clear advantages and benefits when working on a team where global and cultural diversities abound. However, there are also considerable challenges when operating in this manner. Increased global competition, the influence of technology, and the immediate access to global resources have driven massive changes in the way companies develop products, search for talent, and engage customers. Businesses operate in a dynamic, competitive, and ever-changing environment. An organization that resolves to avoid change and remain stagnant over time must accept the risk that it could very well become irrelevant, as other firms grow through change and the disruption of older methods. VTs provide businesses the opportunity to harvest unlimited, unique employee talents and dynamic, specific skills without limitations and across the ends of the earth.

> *Increased global competition, the influence of technology, and the immediate access to global resources have driven massive changes in the way companies develop products, search for talent, and engage customers.*

Given the relative newness of VTs, research in this area of leadership spans only a few decades. Both managers and academics alike are still striving to understand the best ways to work through the many difficulties people face when working in separated environments. There are, however, certain areas of research that may support more effective leadership in virtual work. One example is the psychological contract, which has been demonstrated to be an important behavioral driver in traditional business teams. Furthermore, there are other factors, such as trust, culture, role clarity, issues related to geographic and time zone factors, and the manner and frequency of communications technology usage, that have also been shown to be important to those in VTs.

Given all of these potential complications, any tools that will help leaders of remote teams improve their effectiveness and increase their ability to lead in this environment can be helpful. This book is meant to serve as a practical guide to help leaders succeed and survive the minefield of VT management. To help elaborate each point, the book will follow the story of Mr. Ben Jonas, a fictional vice president of marketing, who has taken on a new job leading a global VT. While Ben is a fictional character, the problems he faces are very real. Each chapter will present a new issue for Ben and will provide a contextual view of each topic presented, interwoven with current academic and practical research findings, while providing helpful tips for today's virtual leaders. The book will illustrate through the case study how Ben makes mistakes in his leadership, so that real-world leaders and readers won't repeat them when it really matters.

CHAPTER 2

The Beginning

Ben Jonas stared at his computer and pondered over the problem that just popped up in his inbox. He had recently begun a new job as vice president of international marketing at a large, Southern California software firm. Although he was very excited about the role, he was also nervous about the challenges that accompanied it. A perfect example of these potential issues was the e-mail message he just received. One of his employees named Jana had asked him exactly what her new job responsibilities would be and whom she would report to now. While these questions seemed trivial on the surface, Ben certainly understood her predicament. Most concerning to him was that he really didn't know the answer.

Ben had worked for years managing the marketing team at a competitive firm and had an industry reputation as an exceptional leader. He was sought out by a recruiter and moved into his current job with the promise of a promotion and a significantly higher salary. He was, of course, delighted, but he was also very concerned about the new way he would be managing his team. His concern stemmed from the fact that only one member of his group of 20 worked directly with him in his office. The rest were remote, virtual workers who were based in other national and international offices. Some of his employees were based entirely on different continents and worked in varying time zones.

While Ben had managed a few virtual workers in the past, they were mostly U.S.-based employees telecommuting from home. To further complicate matters, his new organization was a matrix organization, which meant that other members of the executive team had line access to his group and in some cases could even influence their key performance indicators. Ben would later discover some new challenges directly related to this kind of organization. He began by studying the organizational chart, but there remained many unanswered questions. In the case of Jana, for example, she was a brand manager for one of their core products. Her office was in New Jersey, which put her three hours ahead of Ben's time zone in Pacific Daylight Time. Although Ben was her direct supervisor, Jana was also required to execute tasks for other regional managers, including the local sales and the head of the customer consulting group and R&D. Ben would have to look deeper into the corporate structure and determine how he could best answer Jana's concerns.

One of the significant and immediate issues for Ben was how he could most effectively meet and integrate with his new team. Historically, Ben always held an initial meeting with the group and each individual employee as soon as was possible in each case. He thought these initial face-to-face appointments were of extreme importance in building rapport and trust with his team members. As it turns out, he was right. Ben understood the importance of a cohesive and well-focused team. It is important for any organization to have efficient teams with employees who can work together to provide positive outcomes without major conflict. Each team member can have important objectives that impact not only their individual group, but the organization as a whole (Jane n.d.).

Managing a team within a single, local office can certainly have its challenges. Leaders must deal with varying personalities, ambitions, temperaments, etc., all the while maintaining a vision for the group and driving them toward the overall team goal. However, when the same manager is now thrust into a virtual or geographically displaced team, the complexities of leadership can increase exponentially. These additional complications in virtual management can be overwhelming to even the greatest leader of a traditional team. They can also result in a potentially ineffective and conflictive workforce that destroys project outcomes before the first task even begins. Some researchers have even proposed that diverse working groups can be less effective, while others have demonstrated that diverse teams can actually increase team performance when working cohesively (Maznevski 1994). As a result of these continuing changes in the organizational dynamic, leadership styles are frequently adapted and the old hierarchal approaches replaced with a renewed focus on telecommunications and greater connectivity among team members and management (Siebdrat, Hoegl, and Ernst 2009).

It is important for any organization to have efficient teams with employees who can work together to provide positive outcomes without major conflict . . .

Furthermore, words can have a more powerful impact when working virtually and can often be misinterpreted.

This was the dilemma Ben faced. He had over a decade of solid management experience. His hard work, intelligence, and tenure afforded him the ability to successfully lead his previous team to seven years of increasing revenue and market share growth. It was always easy to pick up the phone or even walk to the next office to handle critical issues. However, now he had to deal with people who he often wouldn't even be able to contact for six to nine hours. Other questions bothered him too. Would the global communication technology work well? Would he be able to effectively motivate his remote employees without that daily contact he was used to? Would he be able to trust them to make decisions while he was asleep at night, and they were in the middle of their work day? Ben had legitimate concerns about his position, and his need for information was immediate.

Ben was a traditional team leader who reveled in the manager-centric and hierarchal aspects of the role. However, virtual teams often render traditional, hierarchal leadership rules useless. Technology is the key to communication, and distance can create feelings of isolation (Johnson 2010). As a result, Ben must learn to develop a greater sense of understanding for each member of his team. The potential breakdown of team coherency and effectiveness can result from ineffective management on the side of an unprepared leader. Contrarily, a well-managed virtual team can foster many positive team outcomes, including increased innovation, cross-functional team knowledge, global diversity, and even improved customer service.

To begin understanding how to successfully lead a virtual team, it is important to consider that distance working can have a profound impact on the human psyche. Furthermore, words can have a more powerful impact when working virtually and can often be misinterpreted. For example, managers may make casual promises or suggestions, without considering the long-term implications of what is being said versus the employee's interpretation. This phenomenon is known as the psychological contract, a term coined by Denise Rousseau in the 1980s. The psychological contract essentially represents an unwritten contract that is developed through a working relationship, and it reflects the concealed emotions or expectations employees may have regarding what they consider a fair exchange between them and their manager or company. In simpler terms, the psychological contract is a mutual, unwritten agreement based on the promises or commitments made between parties.

Understanding the psychological contract can be useful because it can help leaders better understand potential emotional responses to commitments. This is especially true during times of change, when reactions can be exacerbated due to uncertainty. In such situations, a leader must use great caution with his or her words, as repercussions based on a manager's decisions can be significant and can have a long-term impact on how employees adapt to the new environment (Morrison and Robinson 1997).

A huge concern for Ben was the question of whether his leadership style would still be viable while managing a global virtual team across international borders. Leadership can be defined in many ways. Some would say that it is simply a set of skills that can be developed over time, whereas others would argue that leadership is based on the character of a person and can inspire and create a vision for the team. Indeed, leadership is a process in which a manager can motivate, mobilize, and inspire his or her team to focus on a particular goal (Wolinski n.d.). In the past, Ben had debated about whether it is better to lead others through fear, or to take a more loving and caring stance.

Love or fear? Both approaches have been highly studied, and each has its own merit under certain circumstances. In the love approach, the leader inspires his or her team through an employee-centric focus, while the fear method is entirely contradictory in that it is the authoritarian method of management, which gives little credence to input from individual team members (Snook 2008).

After reading some books on management, Ben also thought about whether he was an autocratic, democratic, or laissez-faire leader (Cutajar 2017). Like the fear method of leadership, the autocratic method is manager-centric and puts little to no value on input from the team.

On the other hand, laissez-faire leadership values employee input and minimizes the authoritarian role.

After his investigation, and based on his experience, Ben preferred the democratic leadership style, in which the leader still maintains authority, but subordinate input is accepted (Cutajar 2017). Democratic leadership, also called participative leadership, promotes employee creativity and input, while still stipulating structure from the management (Cherry 2018). The democratic leadership style reflects a balance in which the manager maintains clear control, but still gravitates toward the love approach in that he or she places great value on their employees' input and ideas.

Across his managerial career, Ben also applied the Situational Leadership Model, which involves the implementation of transitional leadership styles depending on varying situations and employee competence and commitment (Northouse 2013). He would at times employ the Transformational Leadership Model, which focuses on leading through transformation and charisma. He did this not only to motivate employees, but also to drive real changing behavior that could benefit them and the organization as a whole in the long run (Reynolds 2015). Furthermore, he would incorporate the Servant leadership approach, which facilitated Ben's general leadership through the emotional and personal connections he made with his subordinates. This was contrary to the fear approach, which places the manager firmly above his or her employees and promotes leadership through intimidation and authoritarianism (Snook 2008).

Ben liked the analogy of nature, where there are places, often on coral reefs, in which large fish and sharks swim slowly with their mouth agape and allow smaller cleaner fish to enter and clean their gills of bacteria and other unwanted parasites. In exchange, the fish get a free meal and they aren't eaten. This process of two species working together for mutual benefit is called symbiosis and could also be an exceptional model for management (Muli-Kituku 2006). Ben learned that whether working in a traditional office or a virtual environment, a leader should consider the symbiotic relationship between themselves and their employees. This is especially true in times of change, as it is a process that can often have profound impact on both sides in ways that are often overlooked (Chu and Fu n.d.). Therefore, Ben found a model to represent the importance of the symbiotic relationship (psychological contract), and a framed copy of it always hung on the wall of his office (see Figure 2.1). Ben understood the importance of people as his most valuable asset and that his management style could impact his team in more ways than he understood (Chu and Fu n.d.).

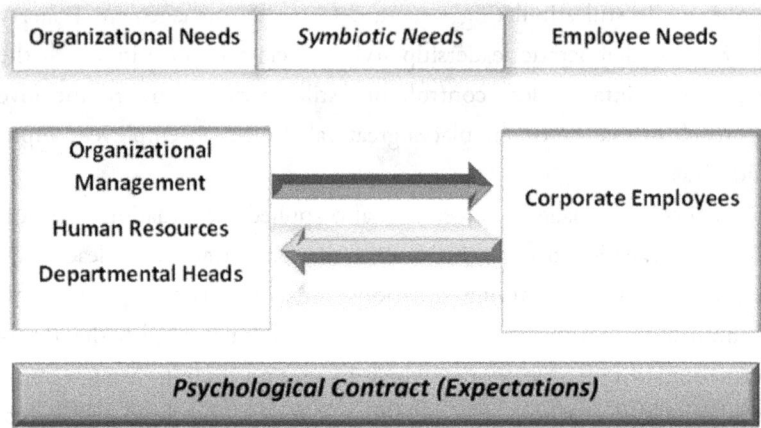

Organizational Needs	*Symbiotic Needs*	Employee Needs

Organizational Management Human Resources Departmental Heads	⟶ ⟵	Corporate Employees

Psychological Contract (Expectations)

Figure 2.1 A simple illustration of the key stakeholders on both sides of the corporate relationship, along with their needs and the ever-present, underlying Psychological Contract that can impact them both (Brady 2014).

As we turn back to Ben's original problem, it is important to reflect on his plan to meet the team face-to-face first. It is fundamental for any manager to weigh the cost/benefit ratio of this decision. Certainly, there is a cost to visiting multiple employees across varying geographies and time zones. One might just consider the financial impact from the organizational perspective, but there is also a personal cost to consider. Traveling to multiple countries would take time away from Ben's family and home and could be physically draining. Yet research and experience support the idea that an initial face-to-face meeting with Ben's team could be a critical factor in beginning well with distant employees (Watkins 2013). Furthermore, leaders of virtual teams rely almost exclusively on technology to communicate and manage the performance of the team throughout the life of a project (Thompson et al. 2000). Ben knows that at the initiation of a virtual team project, it is generally the responsibility of the team leader to bring his or her people together and to provide guidance in reaching objectives, influencing cohesive citizenship behaviors, and pushing them to become a self-managing entity. Accordingly, the manager also has the responsibilities of developing the team and managing performance (Johnson 2010).

Maybe Ben can be an agent of connection and find creative ways to bring his team together and build trust in a more natural manner, similar to the progression in a more traditional, nonvirtual setting (Issacs 2012). Ben understands that an early face-to-face meeting with team members could help alleviate problems down the road. Additionally, managers can maintain a certain level of order and congruency by developing a framework to guide them through better comprehension of the fundamental processes and team directives.

Will Ben's symbiosis model of management be a fit for his new virtual team and project goals? Or are alternative frameworks, like a periodic table approach which segments varying attributes of virtual leadership into a scientific evaluation of elements to increase management effectiveness, a better route to follow (Lipnack and Stamps 2000)?

Managers can maintain a certain level of order and congruency by developing a framework to guide them through better comprehension of the fundamental processes and team directives.

Indeed, Ben Jonas had a lot to think about. While he felt momentarily overwhelmed, he knew that many of his questions would be answered with experience. It was late now, and as he stared into the blue light on his screen, he pondered the very serious issue that Jana had brought up. This, he thought, is a question of roles . . .

CHAPTER 3

Technology and the Roles Game

Ben was in his office staring out the window and wondering what he would do next. He had been very busy in the past few months, traveling across the globe to meet each member of his team, either individually or in meetings. Despite his efforts, he was unable to meet up with every person. In these cases, he was able to set up teleconferences or voice calls with them. This wasn't ideal in Ben's mind, but he felt that at least a contact was important. Of course, while he preferred face-to-face meetings, his travel schedule was exhausting. In the end, he felt it was well worth the effort, as his team seemed excited by his transparency and openness to their ideas.

Now the real challenge began, as Ben would be dealing with his people primarily through technological means. He was about to have a meeting with two team members but was a little confused with the new platform. Ben felt comfortable with his level of digital intelligence (DQ). In the past, his company used basic Skype conferencing for online meetings, but his new organization used newer, more sophisticated tools to communicate with remote employees. Software programs such as Slack, GoToMeeting, and Zoom Video provided many options for Ben to work with his team and communicate in both chat and voice. While they seemed relatively easy on the surface, Ben was still getting used to them. This made his initiation as a manager all the more challenging. He picked up the phone to call the IT group and stood by sheepishly as they explained how to use the software. Effective communication technology is a necessary component for a successful virtual team (VT) integration and leadership.

Throughout history, people have been striving to find new ways to shout at each other and gain attention among their peers (Gascoigne n.d.). Virtual communication simply allows us to do this around the world and without losing our voices. Although working globally through the use of technology can be beneficial, virtual teamwork has not always been possible. The Internet has made profound changes to the way corporations do business. Since 1995, the Internet has been a catalyst for the creation of new ways to conduct business and reach customers. Included in this is the ability to forge teams working in different geographies while focusing on a common goal (Asprey and Cerruzi 2008). Of greater importance, Internet technology has the benefit of improved efficiencies through the reduction of travel costs, enhanced communication capabilities, and increased diversity and talent opportunities (Townsend, DeMarie, and Hendricksen 1998). While most of the world's Internet users reside in North America, Asia, Europe, and Latin America, over the next decade, the Internet penetration ratio across both developed and developing markets is expected to see continued growth, especially through the use of mobile phone technology (CNBC-TV 2013).

Though the continued proliferation of technology provides many great new opportunities in business, one cannot just drop new communications software into an organizational system and assume it will be a magic solution to all company problems. The implementation of new technology can be an excruciatingly complex issue that can result in a loss of both temporal and financial resources if not executed properly. To further complicate the matter, people respond to diverse types of technology differently, so managers like Ben must be aware of this fact as they begin the process of building a new technological platform (Nayak and Taylor 2009). Ben was too busy to do any specific training on the new communication tools at his disposal. He felt confident enough to start working with some of the programs and assumed it wouldn't be too challenging. Nonetheless, in some cases, Ben stumbled through meetings and had problems with his camera and microphone. In one embarassing moment, some of his group had to explain how to change slides and show his desktop in conference. He had read about how to do this, but in the heat of the moment, he forgot and couldn't figure it out. Turns out his DQ wasn't what he thought it was. Despite these minor setbacks, time and experience made Ben a capable user of the new technology tools. Ben learned that the use of technology to connect teams is a journey that requires constant energy and personal development.

For any manager, the hope is that technology will not just serve as a tool, but rather be an instrument to help drive the vision of leadership. Nonetheless, the process of building a successful VT is a tremendously challenging and complicated endeavor. This is primarily because it requires the effective blending of technology, processes, and people. It is not as simple as just setting up and using technology straightaway (Nayak and Taylor 2009).

The implementation of new technology can be an excruciatingly complex issue that can result in a loss of both temporal and financial resources if not executed properly.

Another challenge of remote teams and working in this virtual manner is the limited capability of team members to pick up on nonverbal clues and inflections that are present during face-to-face conversations (Walther and Burgoon 1992). Following the initial application of software, it becomes easier to adjust technology after the team has repeated electronic, text, or voice interactions (Virtual Teams Survey Report 2016). Using a bilateral mode of communication technology can make simple tasks, such as brainstorming and personal discussion, more difficult for some (Follet 2009). In the past few months while Ben had been meeting his team, some employees had expressed that in an environment where nonverbal cues could not be seen, they focused on delivering more concise messages that would resonate effectively with the team. This method can help to facilitate more effective meetings that are more focused and synergistic and thus serve to waste less time (Majchzrak and Malhotra 2004). Furthermore, depending on the communications platform the organization is using, many of these challenges can be somewhat overcome. People can still have visual face-to-face conversations through hardware and software programs such as desktop conferencing, video conferencing systems, Skype, etc. (Townsend, DeMarie, and Hendricksen 1998). This helps people feel connected in a different way and can increase connection between team members. Ben felt comfortable with the level of technology his company incorporated. His main issue was managing the programs more effectively, but even this grew easier over time.

Ben also quickly discovered that some members of his team were more comfortable with communications technology than others. Many of his younger employees not only worked well in this environment, but also fully embraced it. However, some of his managers who had been in the company for years were more reluctant to work in this way. For example, one of his American managers, Ted, used e-mail as his primary communication tool, often writing long notes. Ben tried to push him to use Slack or GoogleDrive more often in his team communications. However, even after many months, Ted continued to spam the team with long e-mails. Ben asked one of his other managers to set up a video conference with Ted and teach him how to use the programs he had suggested, to increase his comfort level in communication in this area. Ted reluctantly agreed and, after some time, finally started to use the programs. While he still sent more e-mails than necessary, he started to improve.

Ben wasn't immune to these problems either. In one call, every time he put his video camera on, the conference would stop working and his voice would get severely choppy. Eventually, Ben told the team to disconnect and call into conference through the phone. Following the meeting, Ben contacted tech support, and irritatingly told them that the system wasn't working. Within a second, the tech support person informed Ben that he had been using a camera resolution that was too high for the bandwidth. After reducing his resolution, the program worked fine. Despite this minor embarrasment, Ben made strides with his use of technology and eventually learned to appreciate the benefit it brought to his team. E-mail, texting, Internet phones, team web pages, and cloud-based connectivity are additional ways that people can communicate across borders (Follet 2009).

The computer company IBM not only used e-mail, video conferencing, and other technology to support its teams, but also utilized selected social networking sites for its employees. This provided them with the opportunity to openly share ideas and collaborate on varying projects (Payton 2010). Similarly, many organizations, including Ben's, use such tools for communication.

E-mail, texting, Internet phones, team web pages, and cloud-based connectivity are additional ways that people can communicate across borders.

E-mail is a very effective, though often overused tool. However, research has clearly demonstrated that using numerous technologies, instead of just one, can help promote better team cohesiveness and trust among team members (Virtual Teams Survey Report 2016). Furthermore, e-mails can be time consuming for both the sender and the reciever. If an e-mail is poorly written or written sloppily and in a nonconcise manner, the receiver can decode the message incorrectly or fail to perceive its core message. This is especially true in a virtual environment (Ferrazzi 2013). As Ben discovered with employees like Ted, e-mail can often be overused and can clutter his inbox. Clearing this out requires a lot of time and effort.

To help reduce e-mail workload, team web pages can be another effective tool. These websites can be a public domain, for example, or they can be Hosted Web Collaboration Environments (Software as a Service). These collaboration sites are more secure and private virtual workspaces that allow global teams to work in an asynchronous manner (work carried out across different time zones). They can also offer real-time conferencing (Woolley 2014). Virtual workspaces, when used effectively, can help reduce confusion as a result of multiple intercompany communication exchanges, while keeping the team in close contact throughout the life of the project (Hill and Bartol 2018). For example, Ben had multiple technology platforms at his disposal. His company used Slack and Google-Drive to manage documentation and text communication. Both of these programs allowed users to share documents and communicate over the Internet, thus facilitating group projects in a VT.

Ben knew, however, that it was extremely important that managers use the technology that would best fit their team objectives. Not only would it be a waste of time, but forcing a team to learn unnecessary new technology could be detrimental to productivity and cohesiveness if it served no real purpose (Hill and Bartol 2018). It can also be necessary to experiment with technology in order to find the right fit for an organization.

It is entirely possible for an organization to become bogged down through the acquisition of new technology, resulting in greater complications and frustrations. Rather, a company should focus on the most effective and efficient technology for their needs and objectives (Boule 2008).

Regardless of the technology used, Ben recognized that it is crucial to keep in mind that technology, like a hammer to a nail, is simply a tool that provides the means for VTs to communicate and collaborate. A hammer on a desk is nothing but a weight. It is how a person swings the hammer that will dictate whether the nail goes into the board or not. Similarly, technology must be utilized in such a way that it will enhance the communication process, not just make it possible. In addition, dispersed team members often find it difficult to measure the time dedicated by other people to a given task. Therefore, Ben implemented a task page where team members could update their individual progress and keep the team abreast of their work in real time, resulting in greater motivation and progress toward their goal (Andrews 2004).

Technology must be utilized in such a way that it will enhance the communication process, not just make it possible.

In time, Ben knew he would adjust to the technology, but he was at least satisfied that his team was ahead of the game, as they already had experience in this area. Most of the team had worked together for many years and were used to some of the tools at their disposal. However, some newer team members, like Ted, who failed to embrace the new software made it difficult at times to integrate the whole team into the process. To increase team communication, Ben set up weekly face-to-face meetings through GoToMeeting or FaceTime and tried to maximize each moment spent with his team.

However, similar to Jana's issue, several other team members had approached him about how they should manage their roles, given that they had many stakeholders to deal with. This was a question that Ben would now have to face head-on. In all his years as a leader, Ben had never seen so much confusion related to job roles. What was really going on here? Was it that the company had done a poor job of communicating job responsibilities or was the organizational structure all wrong? Perhaps it was none of these. Ben set up a meeting with HR to try to better understand the organization and hopefully help his team in the process.

Sadly, Ben's problem is not a unique one. In fact, one of the great challenges of the multinational working environment is the potential for lack of team role clarity. For team members and managers alike, knowing their purpose and having a clear understanding of their role is a fundamental necessity for those working in VTs. This is primarily because while they are working outside the bounds of traditional company life, VT workers often have fewer bureaucratic rules and regulations to guide them in their tasks and they may be relatively disconnected. Therefore, it is particularly important that people working in this way have a common purpose and goal to stay in tune with the rest of the team (Lipnack and Stamps 2000).

So often is the case where one member of a team, such as the manager for example, sees the complete "picture" of the objective, while other members of the team wallow in the mist, uncertain of what they are supposed to do, or how their individual task will contribute to driving them closer to the goal (Ferrazzi 2014). Because of this, an important characteristic of a successful VT is that individuals have a clear vision of both their own roles and how their task will impact the team's overall common objective. Included in this understanding are all role areas, such as time constraints, work priorities, performance expectations, resources, etc. (Juneja n.d.). To drive cohesiveness, the purpose of a team must be a unifying factor that brings together clear objectives, team needs, and the overall corporate strategy (Cascio and Shurygailo 2003).

In addition, it is imperative that VTs and their managers understand the specifics of their compensation and rewards related to their key performance indicators (KPIs) and objectives (Brandt, England, and Ward 2011). While role clarity is crucial to virtual work and may seem like an obvious factor to most people, it may come as a surprise to some to learn that many people who work on VTs feel that they are unclear about what exactly their individual goals are supposed to be. Furthermore, when working virtually, leadership should press their teams to have open conversations with each other to foster communication throughout the virtual working process (Ferrazzi 2014).

A fundamental problem related to lack of role clarity is that it can lead to a demoralized team that delivers subpar performance on assigned tasks.

This can ultimately lead to burnout, frustration, and possibly even termination (Foster 2012). Additionally, lack of information surrounding role clarity introduces the potential for role conflict. Role conflict occurs when two members of a team are unknowingly working on the same piece of a project. Down the road, this can lead to further divergence, frustration, tension, and anger, which can be disastrous to any team, but especially a virtual one (Pazos 2012). Furthermore, this confusion can result in lower job satisfaction down the line (Lyons 1971). Contrarily, clear task and role expectations can help managers enhance employee satisfaction and reduce stress and can provide more time for the manager to focus on other areas of managing his or her VT, such as relationships, for example (Kayworth and Leidner 2015).

It is also important for a VT leader to clearly differentiate specific task objectives from overall role clarity. A manager can help to facilitate a greater level of team collaboration in teams with clearly defined job roles, yet it is also important to guide the team on how to achieve these goals (Ferrazzi 2012b). One of the great benefits of VT work is diversity and creativity, so it is important not to restrict a team member's creative contributions to the team project. Hence, there should be not only clear and concise role and mission guidelines, but also clear measurement parameters to aid the team in their work (Nunes, Osho, and Nealy 2004).

> *One of the great benefits of VT work is diversity and creativity, so it is important not to restrict a team member's creative contributions to the team project.*

Role clarity can become even more convoluted within Matrix organizations, like the one Ben joined. In this case, a single employee may have multiple managers, or a dotted line from another department. Essentially, employees can have two or more managers or departments telling them what they need to do. This ambiguity can directly impact their jobs and even their KPIs, or how they are measured. They may feel like they have no idea who is, in fact, their boss, which can lead to potential power struggles. Over time, this can have negative impact on a virtual employee because it can inhibit effective decision making and even cause inaction among team members (Davis and Lawrence 1978).

It seemed that the organizational culture did not provide Ben with much guidance related to direct structure. After a period of analysis and contemplation, Ben decided that he would give clear and concise guidance around his specific expectations for each team member. He also reached out to other managers who had influence over their roles and, after several discussions, was able to provide Jana and other confused team members with clear role responsibilities. Ben was satisfied that everything was going well and that he had established a solid rapport with his team. However, his next challenge was just around the corner and while he trusted his team, he was soon to discover that not everything was as it seemed.

CHAPTER 4

The Rocky Road to Trust

Ben wasn't happy. He had just experienced his first major disappointment after only four months on the job. He was tasked with developing a measurable marketing plan that would drive revenue and increase market share for the company's main product by 6 percent over the next year. Most of the data he required were already in his hands, but he still needed year-to-date information from Thomas, one of his employees in the EMEA (Europe, Middle East, and Africa) offices. Thomas rarely responded to e-mails, or group chats, and this frustrated Ben. Furthermore, Thomas had now missed two deadlines. When Ben first had a face-to-face meeting with Thomas in the Netherlands, he appeared to be pleasant and easy to work with. Thomas seemed to understand his business, and his team spoke highly of his abilities. Ben came away from his first meeting feeling that Thomas would be a solid and trustworthy employee. However, over time, this image of Thomas diminished, and his lack of responsiveness made things difficult for Ben.

The Oxford Dictionary says that trust is a "firm belief in the reliability, truth, or ability of someone or something," and the "acceptance of the truth of a statement without evidence or investigation" (Oxforddictionaries.com 2018). However, in virtual teams (VTs), trust is often underappreciated, though it may have an even greater importance in this environment (Harrel and Daim 2010). When asked what the most challenging aspect of their role is, virtual leaders often say it is building trust (Settle-Murphy 2006).

As a part of this trust issue, multiple task challenges and socioemotional functions can significantly impact VT effectiveness. More specifically, task-related factors such as communication can be directly influenced by socioemotional factors like trust and cohesion (Powell, Piccoli, and Ives 2004). In fact, research has clearly shown that trust is essential if a virtual leader is to achieve success and permanence within his or her team (Ngo-Mai and Raybaut 2007). When trust is removed from a situation where the team already faces challenges related to geographical and temporal distances, a psychological separation can begin, which can be truly devastating (Jarvenpaa and Leidner 1999). Trust can be impacted by many unforeseen factors in any business team, virtual or otherwise, and this was an issue that greatly concerned Ben. In his experience, trust was one of the most important elements of teamwork. He had worked on many collaborative projects through the years, and he knew the value of trusting other team members to do their part of the work. In his experience, only the teams where members could fully trust each other, and their work, were successful.

Ben was correct in his assumption that trust is an integral part of a successful team. Trust is among the three core foundations of rational choice theory and how people act. Additionally, these include reciprocity and reputation of keeping promises. Within this theory, a rational individual's trust can be enhanced or diluted by the actions and responses of other individuals, such as a manager or colleague. Based on the observed actions, the individual will choose whether to make collaborative actions and decisions. Therefore, based partially on individuals' level of trust in their teammates, their decisions to collaborate or not will be impacted by reciprocal behavior, as trust cannot be built and maintained without solid credibility (Meirhoefer 2008).

The prevailing thought among leaders is that trust is far more difficult to achieve in a virtual setting, because of lack of direct interaction with team members. However, the reality is that this may not be the case. Trust can be developed through different mechanisms in a globally dispersed team. Even within the constraints of temporal and geographic separation, exploratory research has shown that while trust can be squandered and can rapidly dissipate, it can also be effectively created and nurtured within a virtual environment (Jarvenpaa and Leidner 1999). Empirical research has also demonstrated that team reliability is a fundamental factor for building trust in a VT. When team members feel they can count on each other or their managers to consistently deliver on necessary task or role assignments, it can be an important catalyst for building greater trust. Contrarily, unreliability can result in diminished trust (Meyerson, Weick, and Kramer 1996). When people experience a face-to-face interaction, it is easier to develop a visual assessment of other members of their team. In this case, people often pick up on trust indicators such as body language, facial expressions, and daily interactions to help them formulate cognitive decisions about whether they trust others.

> *When asked what the most challenging aspect of their role is, virtual leaders often say it is building trust . . .*
>
> *Even within the constraints of temporal and geographic separation, exploratory research has shown that while trust can be squandered and can rapidly dissipate, it can also be effectively created and nurtured within a virtual environment.*

Nonetheless, despite its importance in a VT, really building trust through reliability takes time. The upside is that through continued successful task completions, dispersed VT members build positive reliability and credibility among their peers and employees and thus can develop solid, trustworthy working relationships (Styer 2010). Ben had already seen this in his team. Most of his groups had already been collaborating for some time and had established a firm trust in each other. They had already worked through many projects and had demonstrated their ability to accomplish individual tasks with the aim of successfully executing a larger team task. Nonetheless, Ben did notice that some groups still struggled in this area and had a more difficult time cooperating with each other.

Swift trust is one of the earliest models used to define trust in a VT. Swift trust puts the focus on the initial component of collaboration in the team, in which preexisting stereotypes and observation of initial behaviors and actions influence trust at the beginning (Ferrazzi 2012a). In simpler terms, a geographically diverse team may have no previous interaction, and thus cannot possibly rely on traditional methods of building trust using methods such as bilateral communication through interpersonal action, for example. Instead, swift trust theory explains that a virtual trust is more likely to be built on categorical social structures and immediate responses and actions of a team community (Meyerson, Weick, and Kramer 1996). It is a trust that is created immediately out of necessity, but yet lacks strength. Swift trust is a survival method that exists because in a virtual environment, certain tasks must be completed and goals must be met, despite the fact that it is entirely possible that many of the team members have never met and communicate only through electronic means. As a result, team members have an instinctual and immediate trust in their colleagues that exists only if commitments are met. It could even be classified as a necessary honeymoon period, where trust must initially be assumed to accomplish team tasks (Ferrazzi 2012b). Swift trust is most applicable in temporary teams, or teams who are working toward a goal that must be completed within a specific time period.

In Ben's case, Thomas made a good first impression in their brief meeting, so Ben had no reason to believe he wouldn't be trustworthy in accomplishing his tasks and a solid employee. Ben had high expectations of Thomas after his initial experience. When Thomas failed to meet his objectives, trust was quickly lost. However, as Ben contemplated this problem, he realized that it would be equally important for him to achieve a high level of trust from his team. He knew he wanted to earn their trust, but how to do it from a distant office was still perplexing.

Indeed, like Ben's issue, for remote team business leaders, the challenge remains of not only developing trust among the team peers, but gaining it from his or her own group. As mentioned earlier, many virtual leaders name trust as the most difficult factor to manage in the working environment. This is further complicated by the fact that when working in an environment with limited face-to-face time, small misunderstandings can quickly grow to be much larger problems (Settle-Murphy 2006). To further confound the problem, each person interprets salient communication cues within the context of his or her own cultural diversity and language without the context of visual cues (Nemiro n.d.). As an example, Ben received the following e-mail from his boss, who was also located in another city:

Ben,

I really need the APAC Q2 market growth report for both products right away! We absolutely need to get this data on time, no excuses. Get it to me before I meet with Larry tomorrow morning.

Lisa.

Ben read the e-mail and his mind started racing. The brevity and forcefulness of the message told Ben that Lisa was clearly rushed, and it even created a trace of doubt that perhaps he had missed a deadline and she might be unhappy. He made her request a priority, found the data, and sent it to her right away. It wasn't until she called him later that day that Ben realized his boss wasn't angry, she was just incredibly busy. Because Ben didn't know his boss well, it was difficult to interpret her personality through a series of brief e-mails. However, this made Ben reflect on his own style of communication with his employees and how he might change his writing style in e-mails.

Quality over quantity is another important rule to consider when thinking about communication in a VT. Research has even shown that teams with higher levels of trust often communicate with predictability. Thus, teams with more predictable communication schedules demonstrated a higher level of team trust than those that didn't (Ferrazzi 2012a). Ben tried to fit weekly meeting schedules with each regional team, along with follow-ups on project reports for each executable task. Managers can also use the strategy of decentralization of power in order to garner trust from his or her team members. Each member of a team can have diverse skill sets that can set them apart from everyone else at varying stages. A leader who appreciates this fact and allows team members who may be experts or have more experience in certain areas to lead could greatly benefit the team and goal attainment.

Ben recognized the value of instrumental embeddedness to team success. Instrumental embeddedness refers to the level of social interactions occurring through the use of relationships utilizing standard protocols of exchange that are connected to specific task goals (Chang 2008). Greater cohesiveness and social responsibility for collaboration can occur in situations where there exist stronger instrumental assistance bonds between individuals on a team. Ben often had open, two-way communication with members of his team. He truly valued their opinions and he knew his limitations in some tasks were surpassed by the ability of others. This was an area where Ben had long ago discovered the benefit of team diversity and collaboration.

A good manager will also use the skills of his or her team to make them leaders among the group in certain areas, while different team members can lead in other areas. The challenge of managing disparities in power, or when one member has greater power or authority over another, is an important one for VT leaders. Effectively managing this disparity across the group can foster greater collaboration behaviors between team members. The utilization of power decentralization minimizes hierarchal authority and thus affords VT managers more flexibility during time constraints. This is especially important given the difficulties that can arise through technological, asynchronous communication methods such as e-mail (Panteli and Tucker 2009).

Another benefit to shared leadership is the potential for management to model best practices and behavior within the team. Allowing team members to lead in this way also affords the manager the opportunity to coach them and increase behaviors that could be more effective and profitable in the long run (Kahai 2011). Ben had experienced this early on in his career, when he had allowed a lower band manager to take over responsibility for a specific, but major part of a branding project. This manager had gained significant experience working closely with the sales group over the years and thus understood the nuances of how their brand could best be communicated to B2B customers. Ben was relatively new to this area, so he allowed his manager to lead the team, which resulted in not only significantly higher numbers for his brand, but also a better relationship with the sales team as well as respect from both the individual manager and the entire marketing group. Using this experience for his current role, Ben started to assess each team member's ability and decided to choose several members in different regions to become local leaders who could lead in specific tasks and responsibilities and voice the concerns and ideas of other team members within their group. By doing this, he empowered his employees to speak their mind freely and also to suggest new ideas that could benefit the entire team.

> *The utilization of power decentralization minimizes hierarchal authority and thus affords VT managers more flexibility during time constraints.*

Of course, none of this shared leadership would be possible without the reliability and accountability of each team member. Like cells in a biological organism, each employee has an important function. When one fails in his or her role, it can impact the entire team. Like what was happening with Thomas, Ben knew that if he didn't get the data soon, he and his team would also miss their deadline, and that was unacceptable. Ben looked at his clock and realized it was already late in Europe, but he decided to pick up the phone and call Thomas. Thomas wasn't too happy about receiving a call during dinner, but he acknowledged that he had fallen behind on delivering his numbers and promised he would send his data by the end of the evening. Ben was satisfied for the moment, but he wouldn't be fully content until he saw the e-mail from Thomas in his mailbox.

While it is important for each team member to provide value initially, what can really be important is how employees follow through with actions to build upon their value and communicate with each other. This is an area where Thomas had failed Ben. It is important because studies have shown that when urgency exists, and it prompts necessary action within the team, trust can actually be developed more quickly (Meyerson, Weick, and Kramer 1996). In one study, separated teams with the highest levels of trust were those that had frequent interaction among the members, either via e-mail or another electronic source (Iaconna and Weisband n.d). Trust cannot be forced and is therefore more complicated to develop as it requires time to grow. It must be reinforced with each individual interaction over the course of a project. Ben learned this early on, and he had always been a people person. He contacted his team members frequently and allowed them the freedom to touch base with him whenever they felt it important, even if this meant after-hours for him. His irritation that related to the inability to communicate with Thomas was a poignant example of how much communication meant to him. He realized that he would need to set up an action item and communicate this point in his next general meeting with the group.

Ben also wondered how else he could develop a quick and strong trust bond with his team. Through research, he came up with four key points that would be useful to him and to other VT managers:

1. Make a promise to an employee, then follow through and make it happen.
2. Build both credibility and reliability with members of the team and other colleagues, and never fail to complete promised tasks or efforts.

3. Keep open-access for all team members throughout the life of the project.

4. In conjunction with step three, maintain continuous and predictable communication schedules with each member of the team, where possible.

Ben pasted these four points on the wall next to his desk. He vowed to read them each day and focus on the importance of each. Ben knew that if he could establish himself as a trustworthy leader to his group, it would greatly increase their chances of being an overall successful team. He was about to grab a quick lunch at the cafeteria, when his phone beeped. He breathed a long sigh of relief when he saw Thomas's e-mail in his inbox. Lunch would have to wait, as he now had the information he needed to get to work and finish the report for his team.

This challenge was certainly an important one, but Ben felt that every day he was learning new ways to build trust in his team. After he sent the report, he grabbed a quick sandwich and his thoughts drifted for a moment to an upcoming direct-to-consumer product campaign they were going to run in Europe. As he went to pick up his phone and call his director in their Berlin office, it occurred to Ben that it was almost 1:00 a.m. there. Ben was frustrated that his request would have to wait until tomorrow. The positive thing was that he knew that if he e-mailed his employee now, the answer would be in his inbox when he woke up the following morning. Ben started typing, wishing he could figure out a way to manage the time difference. Ben was not alone in his disappointment. Managing across geographic boundaries is certainly difficult, but when time zone differences are thrown in, working with a team can become a nightmare. This was a lesson that Ben was about to learn first-hand.

CHAPTER 5

No Time to Lose

Ben was beside himself as he stood in his pajamas staring at the glowing blue screen in the darkness of morning. He hadn't even had a cup of coffee when he reached for his phone and started checking his e-mails. There was a long chain of notes outlining a major issue in the EMEA (Europe, Middle East, and Africa) region. As he searched back to the original mail, it appeared that the advertising firm the company had hired didn't deliver exactly as promised on their new campaign. The remaining e-mails were the resulting fallout. It seemed that because Ben was inaccessible, someone had approved the budget for a rework of the problematic campaign. This infuriated Ben, as he felt that given the fact that the responsible party was the Ad group, they should cover the costs of the delay and relaunch of the campaign. Ben could already tell that it was going to be a very, very long day at work. He immediately started shooting e-mails to his European team and by the time he arrived at his office, his inbox was full again. It was only 8:30 a.m. California time, but it was already 16:30 in London. The workday in Europe was almost done, and Ben was rushing to fix this problem as soon as possible. He picked up the phone and decided to make some calls. As the line kept ringing, he let out a heavy sigh.

Dealing with the temporal or time differences was quickly becoming a massive challenge for Ben. Some days he had to get up at 5:00 a.m. to manage projects, and this created stress for both him and his family. Due to lack of sleep, some days he was tired and groggy. He also felt bad for his team in Europe and Asia, who were often working very late into the night. This made work–life balance difficult and created stress on both sides of the ocean. It often felt like certain members of his team were at a breaking point. Was there something he could do? Could there be some solution to facilitate this process and help drive efficiencies that would limit the impact of temporal differences? Ben had many questions, but, ironically, no time to search for answers. He decided to take an hour of his day to research the problem. Surprisingly, he found that, while there is little a manager can do to change the problem, there are some techniques that can be incorporated that will at least alleviate the issue and make working across time zones more bearable.

The concept of time is a complicated and ubiquitous notion (Sarker and Sahay 2004). Arguably, one of the greatest challenges of geographically dispersed teams is that of temporal separation, or time differences, between multiple international regions. As we have seen in the case of Ben, time differences can cause tremendous stress and difficulty for a virtual team, and many managers struggle with this issue each day. According to an experimental, quantitative investigation called the *Virtual Teams Survey Report*, just over 80 percent of respondents within the study indicated that operating asynchronously across multiple time zones was the biggest hurdle in their team (Virtual Teams Survey Report, 2016).

Surprisingly, however, working across time zones is not all doom and gloom. There can be advantages to working with temporal variance in remote teams. For example, one benefit of working across time zones is that the team can literally be working on a project for 24 hours. Of course, this advantage also presents challenges, as it can be complicated to set up meeting times that are convenient for all members of the team. Additionally, members of teams working within a synchronous (same time zone) environment have the advantage of access to instantaneous information and answers to key questions from their peers, whereas teams working in asynchronous environments do not have the same benefit, which can potentially lead to delay, confusion, and conflict without some form of a temporal coordination mechanism (Montoya-Weiss, Massay, and Song 2017). Also, due to the difference in time zones, the process of decision making can be delayed as there may not be an overlap of working hours. This can result in emotional stress due to the lack of opportunity for synchronous communication (Flynn 2014).

This is what happened to Ben. Had he not been in bed sleeping, he could have quickly solved the problem. However, instead he woke up to find that agreements had been made, projects approved, and actions completed, which created a complicated mess and an extra day of work. This often happens when a member of the team ends his or her workday, and another team member arrives to their office in another continent. The work is continuous, but bad things can sometimes happen. Nonetheless, some of these problems can be lessened by setting up meetings at different hours instead of fixed times, so that the responsibility of working outside of normal hours falls on different members of the team at different times (Virtual Team Builders n.d.).

Accompanying the challenge of temporal separation is the concept of temporal diversity, which relates to the idea that each individual employee has a unique perspective on time management and urgency (Kahai 2011). The reality is that temporal separation can be much more than a simple time difference, but rather it can also be a disparity in culture and temporal perception (Espinosa and Carmel 2004). This can become important when a manager uses temporal leadership in setting up meetings and providing team communications (Kahai 2011). This concept can be imperative, as a leader must understand how to relate high-priority and low-priority tasks, pace important duties, and remind teams about deadlines in a virtual environment where team members across continents may have very different perspectives.

Accompanying the challenge of temporal separation is the concept of temporal diversity, which relates to the idea that each individual employee has a unique perspective on time management and urgency.

One example of the complexities of temporal diversity is the marked differences between monochromatic (linear/low-context) versus polychromatic (high-context) cultures. Monochromatic cultures value timeliness and tend to focus on one task, whereas polychromatic cultures often engage in multitasking and may not be as focused on specific time scheduling (Hall 2000). Furthermore, the context of temporal separation is affected by not only geographic cultural norms, but also functional, organizational, and departmental norms. For example, within a given company, groups such as marketing, finance, human resources, etc., may be working under different sets of processes that can affect virtual teams (Egelend 2010). Given the social context of asynchronous teams, a virtual manager must effectively facilitate temporal coordination of synchronous and asynchronous conversations to help develop stronger relationships within the team (Nemiro n.d.).

A manager should also choose varying meeting times when possible, as opposed to always setting meetings for the convenience of one time zone. This flexibility makes it easier for all team members to connect and demonstrates that the manager has respect for all team members (Chhay and Kleiner 2013). Other possibilities that can alleviate some of the challenges of temporal management of virtual teams include scheduling meetings well in advance (when possible), showing appreciation for those who sacrificed the most to be present within the temporal constrictions of the meeting, attempting to have meetings within the constraints of all time zones, and asking team members to coordinate a time that is best for them (Virtual Team Builders n.d.). Leadership of temporal variance and understanding the importance of individual perspectives on time can result in a much more successful virtual team in the long run (Kahai 2011).

Another important element that can potentially help a virtual team deal with the problem of working across multiple time zones is open access and communication with the manager, so that the manager is open to his or her team and verbal, written, or visual connection occurs with great frequency (Mochal 2007). A virtual manager can even encourage open dissent among his or her team members when they don't agree with the manager or his or her idea. This can be an important tool that demonstrates to the team that when they have their own opinion, they are free to express it (Garrett 2013). In this way, a manager can encourage open communication with his or her team and provide an opportunity for cohesiveness. Additionally, in the modern environment of *e-leadership*, when a virtual manager is open to his or her team, they can be more proactive in setting task goals and monitoring response times and task achievement more closely within their groups through greater communication guidelines and networking skills (Snellman 2014).

Given the social context of asynchronous teams, a virtual manager must effectively facilitate temporal coordination of synchronous and asynchronous conversations to help develop stronger relationships within the team.

Proper planning in the virtual environment is also of incredible importance. This can help virtual teams remain competitive and function more smoothly (Zofi 2011). In addition, regular and open communication and team employee's ability to freely access their manager can help build trust and team cohesiveness (Snellman 2014). Not only does it behoove the manager of a virtual team to allow open access for his or her team in order to increase the richness of communication and facilitate trust building, but it may also provide a greater confidence for team members to emulate this open style of communication across the team and therefore build stronger and more cooperative team relationships in the long run (Ferrell and Herb 2012).

CHAPTER 6

Year-End Reviews

It was the time of the year that Ben hated. He knew that year-end reviews (YERs) were a necessary evil. However, they took up a great deal of time to collect, assimilate, and prepare information about each member of his direct team. Furthermore, he had to read and sign off on each subordinate employee who worked for his line managers. One of the most challenging aspects of YERs was organizing and executing individual meetings with each member of his team. This became a far more complex task, given the geographical locations of each team member.

Ben was a traditionalist when it came to working with people. He knew the importance of performance reviews, and he knew the impact they could have, both positively and negatively, in the overall motivation and satisfaction of an employee's career. He also knew how difficult negative YER discussions could be. He had experienced everything from emotional outbreaks to confrontational behavior with past employees during negative YERs. Those encounters were face-to-face in an office environment. Now he would be meeting people through a screen and discussing their future based on his subjective perspective. Ben had a relatively high level of emotional intelligence and he prided himself on his ability to read people and help them solve issues that they might not have been aware they had. In the past, these conversations were face-to-face, so he could easily see their nonverbal response as he spoke his words. Now, he wondered if he would be able to pick up on the same cues when speaking with someone through a screen half a world away. He also wondered if his team would be as open with him through technology. These were questions that troubled him and even cost him a few hours of sleep.

As Ben started to make his plans, he took comfort in the fact that most of his YERs this year would be positive. Given that this was his first year in the company, this gave him some comfort. To date, his team had done well and integrated with each other and him as their new manager quite well. However, he did have a few problems to iron out. Primarily, his Dutch employee Thomas had developed an attitude since Ben had to force him to send his project out during dinner time. Thomas had expressed to him that he didn't like to work after-hours. When Ben explained that he only called because he was already past the deadline, Thomas became indignant. As part of his YER, Ben would be covering Thomas's attitude toward the team and work. It was serious enough that he considered flying to the Netherlands to have the discussion face-to-face, but unfortunately, he couldn't fit it into his schedule without causing a long delay.

Aside from Thomas's major issue, Ben had to deal with some other small problems with teamwork, deadlines, and internal communication with different employees. Ben's first call was with a young woman named Mary. Mary was an EMEA (Europe, Middle East, and Africa) employee based in Paris, who had an exceptional track record with the company. She was bright, hardworking, and eager to work with her team, and she would be getting a considerable raise. Ben felt that the conversation would go quite smoothly. Overall, his assumption was correct, until the end of their discussion. Mary told Ben that her previous manager had promised her new opportunities in career growth. She had especially been eying the position of Brand Manager for one of their newer products. Ben knew she was qualified for the job, but he didn't know exactly when the position would be opening. After reviewing her career history, Ben was confident enough to tell her that she would definitely be his top candidate for the job, whenever it finally opened up. She verbally agreed and seemed satisfied for the moment.

A few days later, Ben looked out his window, sighed, and dialed Thomas's number with FaceTime. Thomas answered with a chipper voice and smiled. The two exchanged pleasantries and then got down to business. Ben commenced by telling Thomas some of the positive aspects of his performance, such as managing his numbers well. He hoped this would soften the blow before he delved into all the issues related to Thomas's performance.

"Thomas," Ben said, "Your team peer reviews were quite low. Many people said you were delaying their projects by not sending in work on time."

"Ha! That's ridiculous!" he replied defiantly. "They just know that my work is better than theirs, so they're probably jealous. Besides, I turn my work in on time, mostly."

"Well, you may recall that I had to ring you during dinner because I hadn't gotten your file, which I needed to complete my numbers."

"Yeah, I remember. You don't need to remind me. I apologized. Look, I made a promise that I would improve in that area. I've never been late before. It won't happen again."

Thomas was less defensive for the rest of the conversation. He did express his desire to move up in the organization. He said he felt that his previous manager was holding him back from promotion. This surprised Ben as Thomas's service record previously was quite good. Ben promised Thomas that if he demonstrated significant positive development in the areas discussed, he would get him the promotion he had been waiting for. The two men finished their conversation amicably and Ben disconnected feeling quite content that he had accomplished his objectives. He expected to see improvement in Thomas's attitude, but only time would tell.

After a very long week filled with many calls throughout the day, Ben finished his YER meetings. He felt very confident that his team was extremely motivated and ready to start a successful year. What Ben didn't know, however, was that he had made a single critical mistake. It was impossible to see from Ben's perspective at that point in time, but his words could have possibly cost him his most valuable and trusted employee.

CHAPTER 7

The Emotional Game

Ben felt very happy with his job performance so far. His team seemed to be very pleased, and he had hit his primary key performance indicators at work. It was now time for his own year-end review (YER), and he felt confident that it would go smoothly. His boss, Lisa, invited him into her office and they exchanged pleasantries before getting down to business. As he had expected, she praised him on his ability to be a strong leader and hit his initial goals. She commented that he had grown into the role and seemed to grasp all of the main aspects of the job. Ben smiled as he listened to the positive praise of his performance. After a while, she transitioned into the "areas of opportunity" for Ben—the areas of Ben's job that she felt he could improve. While Ben didn't like criticism, he took opportunities for growth seriously and leaned in to listen closely to what his manager had to say.

She told Ben that she felt he could improve in his effective use of some of the technology. Ben agreed with this and he promised to take additional training to increase his efficiencies in this area. *So far, so good*, he thought. However, she then said something that took him completely by surprise. She told him that she felt he could improve his emotional intelligence (EI). Of course, Ben had heard the old buzz term of EI in college, but he really didn't think people still took it seriously. However, his manager explained that EI was an important and fundamental concept and that their company advocated it, even to the point of training managers. Ben's schedule was incredibly busy, so the thought of adding EI training seemed a bit ridiculous. Furthermore, he remained confused as to why she had even brought up the topic.

Ben's supervisor explained to him that a few employees on his team had indicated on their peer reviews that he hadn't fully understood their emotional states, and thus he wasn't as sensitive to their needs as he could have been. Ben was dumbfounded. He had no idea that any employee had already expressed concerns about his ability to lead. In the end, his overall YER was above satisfactory, and his senior vice president (SVP) was very pleased with his performance. He achieved a raise, accolades from the senior leadership team, and a very positive rating, and yet he felt dissatisfied. Several questions nagged him when he walked out of his SVP's office. Among them was who on his team had complained about him, how could EI be a factor here, and what did he need to do moving forward? It was time for Ben to do some internal evaluation and research the truth about EI and what it would mean to him as a virtual leader.

EI is essentially the ability to process emotional information and cues to enhance thought, understand the emotional state of others, and offer a greater level of empathy as a result. EI has also been described as the ability to perceive the emotional state of other individuals through emotive and facial cues. People with high levels of EI generally have greater capacity to perceive the meaning of different emotional states and indications when dealing with others. For example, imagine that an employee is quiet one day and seems somewhat downtrodden. Many people in the office may assume that he or she is simply tired, or some may not even notice any difference in his or her behavior at all. However, a manager with a high EI may immediately observe that something is wrong. The manager might ask the employee questions in an effort to find out what is wrong and try to help. Most employees would likely value this, and in the long run, it could help them build a stronger relationship with their manager. While there has been some debate about whether having higher emotional quotient, or EQ, is a critical requirement for success, few would argue about its value in managing relationships (DeLeon 2015a). Having a high EQ is rarely listed as a job requirement, but there is no denying that EI can have important consequences for a manager and even the organization. Within the United States alone, bad management practices are causing businesses to lose more than $400 billion per year due to declining productivity (Fermin 2017).

Beyond understanding the emotions of others, another key aspect of EI is that it provides individuals with an ability to manage their own emotions. People with a higher level of EI are generally more empathetic and more aware of how their words and actions might impact others around them, and they tend to take time to think before they act or speak. Furthermore, higher EI individuals also tend to focus on the positive, are more self-motivated and more elastic toward change (Rampton 2016).

EI is essentially the ability to process emotional information and cues to enhance thought, understand the emotional state of others, and offer a greater level of empathy as a result.

For example, consider two contrasting reactions in the same situation. An employee who has a solid history at work has suddenly failed to meet his objectives in the last quarter. He approaches his manager with his head hanging low and apologizes, while promising that it won't happen again. An authoritative manager with low EI might immediately raise his or her voice in an accusatory tone, belittling the employee and sternly warning that further failure will result in termination. However, a manager with a high EI would likely respond very differently. He or she might first approach the employee and ask them to explain what happened and why. The manager with high EI might sense that there is something amiss and try to dig deeper to discover what might be a greater underlying problem. He or she might then express a higher level of empathy with the employee and offer to guide and help the person accomplish the tasks with greater efficiency and clarity. When observing this situation as an outsider, it becomes clear which of these two options would likely have a more positive effect on the employee in the long run.

Research has shown that when employees achieve higher emotional engagement from their superiors, there is an increased level of internal psychological job satisfaction (Gunduz Cekmecelioglu, Gunsel, and Ulutas 2012). Additionally, higher emotional engagement from superiors can help employees become more engaged in their roles and responsibilities, reduce stress, and enhance their organizational commitment and overall well-being (Brunetto, et al. 2012).

The more Ben read on EI, the more he realized the importance it held as a tool to be a more effective leader. Still, other questions nagged him. He began to wonder how he could know if he had a measurably high EQ or not? *Forbes* magazine recently proposed four potential danger signs that a leader's EI may be subpar. These are a high level of emotional reactivity, inability to read the audience or the room, failure to preemptively meet with colleagues before presenting an idea or proposal, and the inability to receive feedback (Fermin 2017). Ben reflected on his experience over the last year and realized that he had, at times, been guilty of the second sign, inability to read the room. He recalled a situation where he was making a presentation to his group and continued drudging through the material, even though everyone appeared disengaged during his discussion. He continued speaking while most of the audience had buried their faces in their laptops or cell phones. In that moment, he had perceived their behavior as simply rude. While this may have been the case, he never made the connection that it may have been partially his fault that they were behaving in that manner. If he had been more receptive to the group, he might have changed his speaking method on the spot and engaged the audience more.

> *Research has shown that when employees achieve higher emotional engagement from their superiors, there is an increased level of internal psychological job satisfaction.*

Ben thought back to his early days of adaptive selling when he would speak to customers and change from his original plan to speak with them about more relevant topics. He used to be good at this skill, but he wondered if he had now become complacent. His organizational EI training had taught him that it is important to understand emotional cues. One way to do this was to read faces. He reflected on the moments that he had lost the audience and remembered how bored they all looked. Some yawned, some even fought off sleep as he spoke. All the while, he ignored these cues and kept talking. It began to make sense to him now that this actually was an area for improvement.

Imagine, for a moment, a manager who must meet individually with multiple employees. Each of these employees enters his or her office and after cordial greetings, they sit, seemingly ready to listen and participate in the meeting. But behind the curtain of smiling faces and focused eyes, all involved may have something happening in their lives that can impact their work, their attention, or their performance. One person may be having relationship problems, while another may have health issues. Others may simply have not slept well and thus find it difficult to concentrate. Whatever it may be, a person with high EI may be able to pick up on small cues, or giveaways that could lead them to see that despite a smile, this person is not ready to be fully engaged in the work conversation. A receptive manager might pause and ask, "Is everything ok?" Even employees who choose to not speak about any problems may feel that the manager is more receptive to their needs, or simply that he or she cares or is willing to invest in them emotionally. This in turn could have long-term positive benefit for both the employee and the manager.

Managing emotions can be hard. Managing them in a virtual environment can be even harder. While there is certainly enough evidence to support the idea that higher levels of EI in managers can improve communication and trust between a manager and his or her people, the question remains about how important it becomes in the virtual setting. Ben thought about how difficult it is to perceive someone's emotional state when they are speaking through the phone or sending messages into the dark void of the Internet. Furthermore, there is comparatively little research on the impact of EI in the virtual environment. While many studies have shown that a collaborative culture is a crucial point in cohesive team creativity, for example, others have concluded that EI is an integral part of developing such collaboration (Barczak, Lassk, and Mulki 2010). Nonetheless, some research clearly supports the notion that EI is a crucial component of virtual team success. To bring it a step further, one study concluded that EI could be a solid predictor of the viability of a team and that communication is one important way that EI influences this (Pitts, Wright, and Harkabus 2012).

So, what did the research findings mean for Ben, or any other virtual manager, for that matter? Ben thought about this question for a long time. He took some time to look introspectively at his own cognitive responses to his people in varying situations. From snappy e-mails to gruff responses in meetings, Ben began to think that he could use some coaching in this area. The problem was that he was so busy. It seemed impossible to take every single interaction and focus so strongly on appropriate emotional responses when he was bombarded each day with e-mails, calls, and meetings from people living in different continents. In fact, it never let up. Ben felt like all he did was communicate with his employees, and yet he knew he needed to improve.

Ben finally decided to try to increase his EQ and improve his relationships with his team. His first step was to try to really understand the perspective of whomever he was communicating with, in every case possible. He felt that if he could take even a few seconds more to simply focus and listen, he could really become more attuned to the needs of his people. By doing this, Ben felt he could enhance empathy with their position and therefore become a much better manager. Secondly, because he was so busy all the time, Ben felt like he was always reacting to situations autonomously and without much thought. He just responded naturally to whatever was thrown his way, and he felt like this should be improved. If he could just take a few moments to think before responding to each situation, Ben felt this could not only improve his emotional response to others, but also make him a better decision maker.

Finally, Ben decided that he would try to psychologically withhold immediate judgment in each interaction with employees. Ben knew that changing his behavior would take time, but he felt it was possible to do it. Therefore, he put a reminder note on his monitor with all of these points and promised himself and his employees that he would improve his communication in this way over the next few months. Five minutes later, one of his employees called. She had gone overbudget and was calling to speak with Ben about it. He put his headset on, breathed a heavy sigh, and pushed connect on his computer. Great journeys of change start with small steps, he thought.

CHAPTER 8

The Invisible Contract

Many months passed since Ben had performed his team year-end reviews (YERs). It was now midyear and Ben was again meeting members of his group. Most of his team had performed well, so Ben expected easy discussions overall.

Ben recalled the YER conversation he had with his employee Mary. She was an excellent worker and had been a top performer in the EMEA (Europe, Middle East, and Africa) region. Her marketing campaign idea was extremely successful, and he lauded her efforts throughout the conversation. After expressing his satisfaction with her performance, Ben told her that within the next few months he would give her the chance to be team lead on all things related to regional direct-to-consumer (DTC) advertising. She seemed very excited about the opportunity and told Ben that she couldn't wait to support the team in this area. After the discussion, Ben made a note of what he had said, and then left to prepare for his next call.

As months passed, Ben didn't think about the discussion again until a reminder popped up on his screen. He sighed when he thought about it now. He had been so busy that he hadn't prioritized Mary's leadership opportunity. However, now, after thinking about it, Ben considered how much work Mary already had done. She was so busy with current regional and organizational advertising objectives and controls that she would likely be overwhelmed if he added extra work. He knew she was capable of it, but he also knew she had a busy family life as well. The more he thought about it, the more he considered postponing, or even canceling the plan. He could still send some team members to her for questions, but he decided against giving her the full responsibility of team lead.

The next day, he called her and told her the news. He iterated that she was already very busy, and he didn't feel it appropriate to dump more work on her shoulders. He also preferred that she instead maintain continued focus on her current key performance indicators (KPIs), without the stress of new responsibilities. Naturally, she seemed disappointed, but Ben figured she would get over it soon enough. What Ben didn't know was that he had just created a breach in what is called a psychological contract that he had made with Mary. As Ben was about to find out, this could be a very serious problem.

The idea of psychological contracts is nothing new. Conceptually, the idea of unwritten promises and their potential impact on work relationships has been around for some time. What psychological contract theory seeks to prove is a speculative description of the cognitive connection between a manager and his or her employees (Rousseau 1995). Denise Rousseau, a respected researcher in the area of psychological contract, describes it as the perceptions formed by employees based on the company they work for and concerning the agreements that have been developed through their career between them and their organization (Rousseau 1995). To simplify the concept of psychological contract even further, one could consider it as the psychological anticipation of something based on unwritten, bilateral agreements between employee and employer within an organizational setting (Armstrong 2006). Theoretically, it could also be considered a methodical framework that could be useful to examine the impact of organizational changes on individual employees over time (Storey 2007).

Even hundreds of years ago, political philosophers including Loche and Hobbes mentioned the notion of mental and subconscious interpersonal contracts existing within the sociopolitical environment between individuals and state (Robinson 1996; Wellin 2007). However, in more recent times, organizational and behavioral theorists began researching the phenomenon within the corporate environment (Smith 2012). Chris Argyris was one of the first people to coin the term *psychological work contract*. The original idea was based on the notion that a working relationship is theoretically founded on the concept that when a manager offers sufficient wages and benefits for the job, employees will then work harder and increase their productivity (Argyris 1960). Later the theory was expanded to include the idea of mutual relationships at work. However, Rousseau used quantitative research to increase knowledge of the more individualistic aspects of the contract, specifically focusing on the idea that an employee's behavior can be greatly influenced by fulfilled promises of his or her manager or company (Griffin and O'Leary-Kelley 2004).

To simplify the concept of psychological contract even further, one could consider it as the psychological anticipation of something based on unwritten, bilateral agreements between employee and employer within an organizational setting.

The psychological contract generally forms at the beginning of an employee's career and continues to develop throughout, while new commitments and resulting expectations are forged (Rousseau 1995). One massive research study even found that when employees completed a corporate training protocol on the psychological contract, there was an increase in employee commitment to the organization (Rousseau 2000). Contrarily, research evidence has also shown that when the psychological contract is violated, such as in the case of Ben and Mary, trust, employee attitude, and behavior can be affected, even resulting in divergent behavior on the part of the employee (Coyle-Shapiro, Jacqueline, and Kessler 2002).

Ben had never studied the psychological contract, so he had no idea about the implications of what he had done. He did realize, however, that when he FaceTimed with Mary since his call, she seemed considerably less enthusiastic than she had during their previous meetings. Ben even started the discussion by reiterating how great she was doing and praising her efforts and results within the EMEA region. He told her that on her current trend, she could expect a nice raise at year-end. She smiled, but Ben sensed that she still wasn't satisfied. Remembering his recent commitment to enhance his level of emotional intelligence, he asked her if everything was all right. She immediately brought up her desire to be team lead on DTC advertising. She had clearly prepared for this discussion and gave legitimate business arguments about how she could help the team and help Ben grow his business worldwide through innovative marketing programs.

Ben could see that Mary was passionate about the topic, and he knew she would do well. However, he still felt uncertain about whether or not he should give her the extra responsibility. He knew that she would need to be further compensated for the role, but now he wasn't sure the budget would allow it. Therefore, he promised her he would consider it again and look into the viability of it. Still not satisfied, she reminded him that he had promised her it would happen at their YER. This comment took Ben by surprise. He remembered that he had mentioned it as an idea, but he didn't recall actually using the word *promise*. Their conversation ended seemingly well, and Ben started to look into what he should do. After having a discussion with Finance, Ben realized that he wouldn't be able to pay Mary the extra bonus for the work unless he cut spending in other areas. At the moment, he needed every cent where it was, so he wasn't willing to make the sacrifice. As a result, he sent her an e-mail informing her that he was sorry, but it would not be possible to create and assign her the lead role at this time. She never responded.

Ben's failure to fulfill his commitment is not an uncommon practice in management. In fact, one study demonstrated that many organizations across multiple industries frequently break promises with their employees. Indeed, in the study group, almost 69 percent reported that they experienced a breach of the psychological contract within the last 10 days leading up to the survey (Conway and Briner 2002). Ben felt that he had made a simple and innocuous statement to Mary. However, to her, Ben had made a promise. In Ben's mind, he had an idea about how great it would be to have her lead the team on a special project, but it didn't work out. In Mary's mind, Ben *promised* her an exciting opportunity to develop her leadership skills and grow in the organization, but he failed to deliver. Ben was learning that words can sometimes be complicated.

The psychological contract can have many perspectives. To begin with, the employee perspective might be constructed by different factors. These might include future career prospects, perceived job security, rewards, and generous compensation based on work completed, among others (Davidson 2001). Some have even implied that the very nature of an employee/employer relationship can be entirely dependent on the constructs of psychological contract (Welsch 2003). Ideally, a work relationship should formulate a solid and stable schema that continues to flourish as the relationship develops over time.[15] Schema could be defined as the intellectual process by which knowledge about a certain stimulus or information, such as a situation or an interaction with an individual, is organized cognitively (Fiske and Taylor 1991). Furthermore, the psychological contract itself can be broken down into two different facets: the relational and the transactional (Rousseau 1990).

The transactional side relates to the expectation of monetary payment as a reward for specific behavioral actions within the company or for the given job role (Woodruffe 1999). While the transactional contract is more ego driven and individualistic, the relational contract takes a long-term perspective and instead emphasizes career development and therefore focuses on a different set of behavioral approaches (Thompson and Bunderson 2003). The problem is that as a result of changes in the global economy and poorly managed organizations, the psychological contract has had a recent tendency to trend more toward the transactional approach (Herriot and Pemberton 1995). This can have very important implications in the relationship between an employee and his or her organization, which can influence attitudes such as lack of trust, lower job satisfaction, and diminishing employee motivation (Herriot 2001). To make things worse, oftentimes the transactional approach is based on fear-focused leadership, which can further isolate employees and promote continued loss of trust. Contrarily, employee-centric leadership that demonstrates commitment and concern toward the team and their career expectations can promote trust and promote creativity, higher levels of teamwork, and better overall results (Mackay 2010).

While he tried to listen to Mary's concern, Ben simply failed to understand the importance of the commitment he had made to her. By telling her she could be in a leadership position, he was effectively promising her an opportunity for career growth, which was a tremendous motivation for Mary. Not only had she internalized the idea that she would be given this additional role, but she also spoke with her family and friends about it. She began to formulate how it might impact her future within the organization and even in her long-term career. Yet, all of this was shattered when Ben rescinded on what he had said. His intentions were good, but he entirely missed the mark and was now just beginning to see the consequences of his actions.

Aside from the transactional and relational psychological contracts, some researchers believe that there are two other different types of contracts. The first, called the transitional contract, is founded in the unseen organizational and socioeconomic changes that can suddenly arise and contradict the initial edicts of the original contract. The second, called the balanced contract, is indicative of an open-ended agreement that relies primarily on employee career development, organizational success, and the precepts for the mutually beneficial growth of the manager and employer relationship over time. The balanced contract is similar to the symbiotic approach, in that the outcome is mutually beneficial for both parties. It is the balanced contract that should be most prevalent in the modern-day organizational setting (De Jong, Schalk, and De Cuyper 2009). Indeed, much of the importance of the contract may be founded upon the prevalence of reciprocity in human culture, and the necessity to promulgate the notion of balance in the context of ongoing social exchange norms between people in the business context (Coyle-Shapiro, Jacqueline, and Parzefall 2008).

What Ben needed to realize is that if he had honored his commitment to Mary, he could have seen benefits far beyond her support of the team. Mary had an expectation of leadership and if she had been given the role, she would have been fully engaged in it, despite the extra work. Her perspective about the organization would have been positive, and her trust in Ben as a leader would have increased substantially. This in turn could have increased not only her motivation, but the team's as well. However, after Ben breached his commitment with Mary, these possibilities essentially went right out the window, leaving Mary in a very different psychological state.

The problem for Ben and other managers in similar situations is that they may not even realize that the significance of the psychological contract goes far beyond employee attitude. Honoring commitments made with employees can potentially increase levels of employee retention as well as driving increased productivity (De Vos, Meganck, and Buyens 2006). Leaders may forget the important fact that the psychological contract and specifically informal or verbal commitments made to employees are essentially internalized agreements that employees subjectively perceive as promises made to them by leadership. The thought is as often as simple as, *If I do X, then my company will give me Y.* Failure to recognize this could have a devastating impact on employee perception of trust and other factors, as well as diminishing their relationship with the manager and the company (Turnley and Feldman 1998).

Honoring commitments made with employees can potentially increase levels of employee retention as well as driving increased productivity.

There exists a lot of evidence supporting the idea that the psychological contract can impact employee behavior. However, many researchers have even postulated that it can also have a powerful effect on productivity and ultimately business results (Wellin 2007). Part of this stems from employee motivation, which can be extremely important for achieving team goals. Because it is an important part of the foundation in which employee behaviors are based, motivation can push employees to go above and beyond their normal KPIs and give them the desire to work harder and deliver more than their objectives warrant (Pintrich and Schunk 2013).

Research has repeatedly shown that employees base their reciprocal work efforts within the organization on the fulfillment of corporate career promises and their subjective assessment of organizational incentives, thus adjusting their own psychological contracts with their company over time (Coyle-Shapiro, Jacqueline, and Kessler 2002). In addition, employees view psychological contracts as an indicator of corporate behavior because they perceive management follow-through as an indication of whether or not they are being treated fairly by the company. This perception of fairness can have a direct impact on employee behavior within their job role (Jackson and Wielen 1998). As in the case of Ben and Mary, promises made at the beginning of a new relationship can be crucial because they may ultimately determine the core essence of the psychological contract throughout the employee's career (Tomprou and Nikolaou 2011). In one example, a study of 340 bank employees demonstrated that the commitments of the psychological contract influenced worker motivation and had a significant influence on attitude (Lee and Liu 2009). In today's growing, global economic environment, the psychological contract is a fundamental tool for effective leadership in organizations that focus on high employee commitment and high performance (Burack 1993).

Four months had passed since Ben's last discussion with Mary about the leadership role. During this time, he noted that she appeared to be more disengaged than before. Normally in meetings, she had been very active, while contributing many relevant thoughts and ideas. However, since the last communication about the role, she was far quieter. She had even missed a deadline, which was something that she had never done before. One of Mary's team members even confided that she seemed far less enthusiastic at work, and she was concerned that Mary may be having problems at home. Ben too was getting concerned. He wondered if it was all because she was so disappointed about not getting the role, or if her recent lackluster performance was due to something else. He decided that it was time to speak with her in person. He had already planned a trip to Europe to meet with other clients. Now he could do both. He called his administrative assistant and requested that she book him a flight to Paris after his initial meetings. Perhaps, he thought, it was time to reevaluate his decision.

Mary was experiencing some of the early cognitive effects of a psychological breach. She had worked many years at the company and had always looked forward to each day in the office. However, her career was a major focus. Ben, she thought, was an okay manager. However, he really disappointed her when he backed out of his offer for a leadership opportunity. This was not the first time a manager in the company had promised her a chance at a leadership role and reneged. Just over a year before, the manager who preceded Ben told her she would be getting a promotion as director of product marketing for her brand. She was very excited about it, until he left and was subsequently replaced by Ben a few months later. The director opportunity was snatched up by a junior marketing person in the United States in the process. Mary shrugged it off and instead focused on doing well in her current role and demonstrating her skills to her new manager. During their YER, he clearly noticed and offered to reward her efforts with the leadership opportunity. When he broke his word, though, she was angry. It seemed to her that this company was full of lies and false opportunities. Thinking about the limited career opportunities she had, Mary started looking elsewhere and promptly made acquaintance with several recruiters. In her mind, the sooner she got out of this sinking ship, the better.

Sadly, cases like Mary's happen all the time. Many studies have shown that breaches of the psychological contract can severely impact not only the employees involved, but also the organization itself. The psychological contract is a two-way street, so when a commitment is made, both employee and employer should honor it. However, a violation occurs when either party fails to deliver on the perceived personal or career promises stated within the original context of the agreement (Robinson and Rousseau 1994). Some people believe that the word "violation" in this context is too strong because many contractual breaches are relatively minor (Morrison and Robinson 1997). However, a true violation of the psychological contract goes much deeper than simple unmet expectations in a given situation. Rather, a violation occurs when a promise is made by one party and the other party perceives that the other group is unwilling or unable to fulfill their side of the promise (Vardi and Weitz 2004).

Regardless, serious violations of the psychological contract can create a severe loss of motivation to work and, in the worst cases, promote employee thoughts of getting safe, getting out of the company, or getting even. Getting safe, in this context, implies that employees will do the absolute minimum to not attract positive or negative attention to themselves. Thus, they will simply fly under the radar and wait for a better opportunity to arrive. Mary, for example, had entered this phase. She no longer made efforts to draw attention to herself in meetings or teleconferences, and she did the minimum required for her job, with little enthusiasm. She wasn't looking to get fired, but at the same time, she had lost her dream of getting promoted. When other opportunities don't come around within the company, the third step of the process comes into play—getting out. One of the recruiters contacted Mary about an opportunity with a competitive company. She had heard negative things from others about the work environment in the proposed company, but her emotional response and loss of trust resulting in the second contractual violation with her company pushed her to accept the interview anyway. It might have seemed irrational at the time, but Mary wanted more for her career, and she was frustrated.

In the final stage, when the situation is really bad, some employees feel that they must get even with the organization for breaking their promise. This is the most dangerous attitude and often involves the desire to somehow "hurt" the organization through sabotage or disruption (Doyle 2003). Despite the possibility of inducing these behaviors through broken promises, one study indicated that 50 percent to 80 percent of company employees feel that their organization has not fulfilled its promises and obligations (Turnley and Feldman 1999). Many times, a violation or breach occurs due to reneging of corporate or leadership promises, like what happened with Ben. In other cases, breaches occur because company leaders are aware of their promised obligations, but for whatever reason, they simply fail to or are unable to fulfill them (Morrison and Robinson 1997).

Another reason psychological contract breaches occur is cognitive incongruence. In this situation, two involved parties have entirely different perceptions about the terms of the mutual obligations referred to in the original contract. Many studies support the notion that breaching psychological contracts correlate with negative behavior on the part of the employee (Griffin and O'Leary-Kelley 2004). Another issue is that the psychological contract is emotionally binding and often includes a perceived sense of entitlement. Therefore, a violation can be a negative and palpable experience for each party (Vardi and Weitz 2004). However, the true implications and results of a breach in contract are often very subjective and therefore difficult to accurately measure.

One factor that helps remove some of this ambiguity is trust. An employee's level of trust in their organization, or manager, can impact their perception of the contract at its initiation. Studies have shown that the level of trust an employee has in his or her company or manager can also directly impact how they perceive a psychological contract violation (Robinson 1996). Along with continued academic research of this concept, companies have started to implement their own formalized management training programs with the aim to increase awareness in the importance of the contract in leadership (Burack 1993). The psychological contract can be an effective instrument for delivering a structured framework that could help examine the cognitive relationship that exists between leaders and their people, as well as understanding how corporate changes impact employees (Johnson 2010). More importantly, as the contract has been demonstrated to directly impact employee behavior and commitment, it is important for corporate leadership to carefully consider promises before they are made (Coyle-Shapiro and Kessler 2000).

What we have discussed thus far relates primarily to the psychological contract in the traditional team setting. But what about in the virtual team environment? As previously noted, the absence of team commitment can have very damaging effects for trust and other factors on a virtual team (Snellman 2014). For virtual managers and their employees, the psychological contract can have a very important impact on what employees perceive as fair for themselves at their job. This, in turn, can directly impact both motivation and employee behavior (Jackson and Wielen 1998). On the positive side, fulfilling promises stated in psychological contracts has been shown in research to help explain trust behaviors in the virtual working environment (Piccoli and Ives 2003). Studies consistently reinforce the importance of congruency of the psychological contract as it relates to perception between both parties. This is especially true when specific constraints of obligations and expectancies between both company and employee are considered. Doing so generally promotes positive employee outcomes (Kotter 1973).

While such ideas seem great on paper, managers really do need to be cautious and choose their words wisely. Contract violations can ultimately be perceived differently in a virtual setting, greatly damaging trust (Davis and Todd 1982). While managers may be the contract violator, employees also may fail to live up to their agreements with management.[51] A big part of this issue comes down to fairness. Virtual employees already have relatively limited access and connectivity with their manager. Therefore, in the virtual environment, employees' perceptions of fairness may be one of the key ways they can determine the intentions of the organization and their supervisor. Furthermore, their cognitive perception of fairness can dictate how they behave in their work environment.

According to a research study, employees who felt they were treated fairly according to the constraints of their psychological contracts with the company were more likely to commit to positive working behaviors, including going beyond their normal required tasks for the job. On the other hand, virtual workers who experienced a breach of contract were more inclined to exhibit negative attitudes and poor work behavior (Jackson and Wielen 1998). Another challenge for corporate leadership is the fact that it is far more difficult to instill a corporate identity with employees who work in a virtual environment. Lack of corporate identity can result in diminished loyalty from the employee perspective, which can in turn continue driving the organizational trend of moving from relational psychological contracts to more transactional ones (Harwood n.d.).

Ben was still perplexed. He wondered how one missed opportunity could have such a strong impact on a great employee like Mary. Before their meeting, he decided to call a good friend who managed a tech firm in California. He explained what happened and asked his friend what he thought. The friend told him that it was likely more than just a job issue. Mary wanted to grow in her career, even if it meant working more hours. He also said that she likely felt jaded because Ben had promised her the role and then he reneged, which likely killed her trust in him as a leader. After hearing this, Ben finally started to understand that it could all be his fault. He hung up and began to formulate a plan. The first thing he was going to do was speak to her and allow her to be entirely open about her feelings. Then, he decided, if she is willing to do the work, he would offer the role he had promised again, starting immediately. A few hours later, Ben walked into the Paris office and saw Mary waiting in a conference room with some papers and a glass of water. He entered the room, shook her hand, and exchanged greetings. He sat down and was about to start, but before he said another word, she spoke.

Another challenge for corporate leadership is the fact that it is far more difficult to instill a corporate identity with employees who work in a virtual environment.

"I'm sorry, but I quit." Ben was dumbfounded. Mary was one of his best employees, even when not performing to her fullest. She immediately explained that she had been tempted by a recruiter and another company offered her a job with a slightly higher salary and, more importantly, a bigger title. Ben tried to counteroffer, but he knew it was already too late. Mary had mentally disconnected from the company. When Ben asked her why, she explained all the reasons, including the issue related to the promised leadership role. After their meeting, Ben started to look into the importance of promises in the workplace, even casual ones. He decided it was time to make some new ground rules. In the virtual setting, words can be spoken and promises made. However, there are two important things that virtual leaders need to consider when making promises, even in informal conversation with their employees.

1. Managers should clearly understand the career goals of their employees and only make promises about employee career development that can be fulfilled by themselves as well as the organization, whenever possible.
2. When the employee fulfills his or her work or performance obligations that were tied to career development promises, the virtual leader must follow through and deliver on the promises made to the employee.

Many studies have shown that the psychological contract can be a fundamental tool in managing relationships in a performance-based organization (Burack 1993). Remote leaders can certainly make mutually beneficial promises for their employees, but they should never be empty words. Ben learned the hard way that pulling out of commitments can have long-term and difficult consequences for a virtual team.

CHAPTER 9

Filling the Void

Ben was now facing a serious problem. One of his best employees had resigned, and he needed to backfill her position as soon as possible. Leaving EMEA (Europe, Middle East, and Africa) without a marketing head could prove to be costly in both the short term and long run. Their group had hired a consultant in the meantime, but the cost was astronomical. Ben needed to work fast and he was about to do something he had never done before. His company had a recruiting firm that they used for filling European jobs, but he hadn't been impressed so far with what they had offered. On the other hand, a colleague had recommended someone he had worked with in the past. Ben was about to meet him virtually, but it would be the first time he had interviewed anyone on Skype before. Logistically, it wasn't ideal, but it was the only way. The local time in Paris was 16:00, while Ben was going to take the call in his house at 7:00. At exactly the expected time, Ben's computer rang that familiar tone and he picked up the video call. He hoped this guy was good, because the urgency of the situation loomed over Ben's head.

Hiring for a virtual team can have its challenges. To begin with, the manager will likely have to rely on technology for the interviews. Secondly, it's just not the same when one is on the phone, or looking at a screen versus meeting face-to-face. It can be harder to decipher important visual cues during the interview, and distractions are more of a problem, such as e-mail notifications popping up in mid-sentence. A leader may have to rely heavily on local managers to meet the candidate and give their assessments of his or her ability. Another problem is the potential for increased costs versus a local candidate. For example, if a candidate makes it to the final interview, the virtual leader may actually want to meet him or her face-to-face before making the final decision. This decision can incur added financial costs from hotel, airfare, food, and any other required transportation. While choosing a solid person may be challenging, it is an absolutely crucial step in being a successful leader, especially in the virtual environment.

In any situation, a bad hire can be a very costly and time-consuming problem. Hiring the wrong person can bring financial, temporal, and psychological costs to a leader. A bad employee can bring down financial results due to lack of performance and/or inability or unwillingness to learn. The new hire may require additional, costly training programs to help maneuver through rough patches, and there may be heavy recruiting costs if the person is so bad that termination is necessary. Furthermore, bad hires can have the manager spending extra time reviewing basic responsibilities with them, helping them improve their performance, or coaching them through continuous failures. Finally, a bad hire can cause psychological stress for both the manager and the other members of the team. In the worst-case scenario, a bad hire can create a toxic environment and demoralize the team. Some may even wonder why the person was hired when they felt more qualified for the role. Hiring the wrong person can create such friction on a team that it could damage not only the reputation of the leader, but also that of the firm in some cases. One study reported that managers spend 17 percent of their time dealing with poor employees. That basically amounts to nearly a full day each week that the managers could have been doing more productive work (DeLeon 2015b).

Following his phone call, Ben took a moment to evaluate the discussion. The candidate had an excellent background and handled himself very well on the phone. His qualifications made him an ideal candidate for the marketing tasks required in the role. Furthermore, Ben was pleased with how he handled the discussions through an online forum. While he was concerned about how effective an interview would be over Skype, Ben felt that he was still able to assess the candidate well. Furthermore, it allowed him to see how well the candidate managed the discussion through communications technology.

Still, there was one small issue that nagged Ben throughout the call. The candidate had excellent managerial experience in local and more traditional teams. However, he had never managed teams on different continents and across major differences in time zones. He wondered how the candidate would handle the stress of having limited access to information at times, while waiting for workers on other continents to wake up. Furthermore, Ben wondered how responsive he would be to issues in the United States, when they might not have much direct relevance to his team. Ben knew that hiring the right person wasn't just about offering up money and hoping someone will fit the bill. Would the candidate's lack of experience with geographically dispersed teams be a major challenge? Ben wondered, and he planned to discuss it in detail with the candidate in the next call.

When hiring new people, money offered is a standard, a commodity, but talent is not. It's about finding the right person for the job. It is so important to find a person who not only has good credentials and experience but also has the right attitude, talent, and fit for the team (Bagley 2013). In the virtual environment, this can be even more challenging. Given the difference in work environments and lack of direct face-to-face communication, additional skill sets are required for virtual team hires. Various issues must be considered. Is the candidate motivated to work in an environment where his or her supervisor is not present? Is the individual able to cope in situations where he or she may not receive immediate feedback from the team or the boss? Can the person adeptly manage communications technology?

Another key issue is whether the candidate can properly prioritize work. The individual may be inundated with e-mails and potential projects, but will he or she have the skill to understand which should be given high priority versus those that can be managed at a later time (McKeegan and McKeegan 2015)? Another key factor to consider when hiring virtual managers or team members is their ability to work with teams and, more importantly, their reliability when managing tasks. As mentioned earlier, reliability is a fundamental factor in building trust in the virtual environment. Finally, candidates who work in an environment where their colleagues can come from anywhere in the world should have cultural sensitivity and be open to different ways of working.

Ben's second call went well. The candidate expressed that while his team was mostly local, he did have some members who worked in other European countries. He, therefore, understood the complexities of working in a virtual environment and welcomed the challenges that accompanied them. Several other managers met with the candidate, but given the importance of the position, Ben felt that he should meet him face-to-face. Ben's administrative assistant arranged for the candidate to fly in for a day and meet with Ben.

Candidates who work in an environment where their colleagues can come from anywhere in the world should have cultural sensitivity and be open to different ways of working.

After spending the day with the candidate, Ben decided to make an offer. He felt that the candidate could be a great fit for the team. He knew, however, that the candidate would initially require some additional training and coaching around working virtually with vastly displaced teams. Still, Ben was comfortable with his decision. Would it payoff though? Ben knew the importance of a good on-boarding for new employees. He was fully aware that the better integrated the employee was, the more satisfied he would be in his job. Only time would tell if Ben had made a good hire, and time can be a tricky subject.

CHAPTER 10

What Is Job Satisfaction Anyway?

Ben was staring blankly at his monitor at the end of another long day. He noticed how many post-it notes had accumulated around his monitor—phone numbers of contacts, reminders, to-do lists, and some random messages to himself that made no sense to him now. Ben started to take them down, when one caught his eye. It was the reminder about his emotional quotient (EQ), and it brought him straight back to his year-end review (YER). It read, "1) Focus and listen more, 2) Think before responding, 3) Withhold immediate emotional judgement." Ben had promised his employees that he would improve in these areas over the next few months after his YER, and those months had now passed.

Had Ben improved in these areas and ultimately enhanced his EQ? His exchanges with Mary resulting in a breach of psychological contract may suggest that his listening skills and his thought processes before responding could be improved still. Mary was an example of an employee who ultimately had low job satisfaction, which could at least partially be attributed to deficiencies in emotional engagement from her superior. Ben wondered if he had other employees who weren't fully satisfied with their jobs.

Ben mulled over the issues around his EQ and felt he had learned from his exchanges with Thomas and Mary and was implementing the goals set out on his reminder note. Thinking about his YER with Mary also got him thinking about YERs in general. Of course, as Ben was a traditionalist, he knew the importance of YERs and their impact on overall job satisfaction and motivation, major factors in terms of an employee's career prospects. Then Ben thought to himself, what is job satisfaction anyway? We all have our ideas about the key features that define job satisfaction, and there are plenty of theories and research out there to highlight those features, but Ben was at a loss to come up with anything off the top of his head. One obvious avenue for clarification on what job satisfaction is could come from upper management itself. Senior leadership should routinely measure employee job satisfaction to ascertain the effect of any company operations and changes that might adversely affect employees.

Ben e-mailed his boss, Lisa, to see if the company had any archived employee job satisfaction questionnaires that had been used in any previous large-scale employee surveys. She responded quickly to say that there were none.

> *Senior leadership should routinely measure employee job satisfaction to ascertain the effect of any company operations and changes that might adversely affect employees.*

During the conversation with Lisa, he volunteered to do research into job satisfaction and come up with a questionnaire to measure it in future company surveys of employee morale. At first Ben thought that he could delegate this extracurricular activity, or at least part of it, to Jana. However, he knew she was stretched as it was without adding another task to the mounting tasks she already had, so he reconsidered. He would have to do this research on his own time.

Back in his college days, history was one of Ben's favourite subjects. So his initial research into job satisfaction allowed him to go back to the 1920s and work forward from there. This made his task more enjoyable. In the 1920s, job dissatisfaction (Mayo 1988) was the focus when employees were surveyed about their work. Negative emotions, including anger, fear, and suspicion, were assessed. The frequency and intensity of these negative emotions were a driving force in the rise of labor unions. Later in the 1930s it was acknowledged that job satisfaction can be affected by job-related factors and employee individual differences (Hoppock 1977). This discovery led to further research of why some occupations had happier workers as compared to others. Along with the occupation itself being a job-related factor, employer concern for workers was also identified as an individual difference factor that influenced employee job satisfaction (Hoppock 1977). Studies revealed that when more attention is paid to employees, and they see this attention as positive, attitudes toward supervision improve, which can lead to increased productivity. This impact has been referred to as the Hawthorne effect (Landsberger 1958).

In the 1950s, a "two-factor" theory (Herzberg, Mausner, and Snyderman 1959) emerged that recognized the influence of intrinsic job-related motivation versus extrinsic job factors. According to the theory, job satisfaction is linked to reductions in absenteeism and turnover intentions, among other positive outcomes. Interesting work challenges the employee, thus satisfying his or her intrinsic motivational needs, while good pay and work conditions would satisfy extrinsic "hygiene" needs (Maslow 1970). Ben knew that Mary's hygiene needs had not been met, and that negatively impacted her motivation.

Critiques of the "two-factor" theory that followed resulted in a move in the 1970s toward recognition of the concepts of valence, instrumentality, expectancy, and equity as determinants of job satisfaction (Lawler 1994). Ben processed these technical terms and came up with a more straightforward explanation. Job satisfaction is achieved if the employee gets from the job what he or she believes is deserved. Again, Ben knew Mary had not gotten what she thought she deserved—the promotion promised to her.

The valence, or value, aspect of job satisfaction (Locke 1976) seemed pivotal to Ben in the definition of an employee's job satisfaction. For example, if the employee valued pay, then a pay raise would have a major positive influence on his or her job satisfaction, but pay is not always necessarily the most important thing to an employee. If an employee does not value the opportunity a promotion provides, then that opportunity, if it comes along, would not strongly influence his or her job satisfaction. Ben felt that in future YERs, he could tease out what each member of his team valued in terms of the job and try to establish goal commitments (Locke 1976) based on those valued aspects to ensure continued satisfaction. Ben vowed that he would not make the same mistake he made with Mary. Any promises made on his part in terms of these goal commitments would be delivered on.

When more attention is paid to employees, and they see this attention as positive, attitudes toward supervision improve, which can lead to increased productivity, in other words the Hawthorne effect.

Ben asked himself the question "What are these valued job aspects?" This brought him out of his historical journey through the development of theories related to job satisfaction to a search for what makes a job valuable to an employee in a virtual setting. Investigations into quality of work life (QWL) stood out as an area of research that could provide him with the answers he needed.

So far Ben had focused on the attitudinal aspects of job satisfaction, where it is assumed that motivation derived from positive job satisfaction leads to improved job performance (Spector 1997). However, job satisfaction can also be an important aspect of an employee's psychological well-being (Arnold, Randall, and Patterson 2016). Ben realized that job satisfaction is linked directly to occupational health and QWL. Ben's company had made some big changes over recent years to address occupational health issues, resulting in the current Employee Assistance Program. Be that as it may, the company had not surveyed its employees in terms of job satisfaction, which was Ben's task at hand. Through research, Ben found that surveys relating to job satisfaction could vary widely: a single question on how satisfied the employee was; multiple statements relating to job satisfaction where set responses, strongly agree to strongly disagree, were provided for the employee to choose from; or a facet approach where various aspects/facets relating to job satisfaction are measured by sets of statements relating to each aspect. If he were to recommend a QWL survey incorporating job satisfaction and related aspects, the facet approach seemed most relevant.

Ben's searches for QWL and occupational health employee surveys led him to the Centers for Disease Control and Prevention (CDC) website (The National Institute for Occupational Safety and Health n.d.). In 2002, the National Institute for Occupational Safety and Health (NIOSH), in agreement with the National Science Foundation, had been able to add QWL questions to the General Social Survey (GSS) of U.S. households, with a slightly modified version of the survey administered again in 2006 and 2010 (The National Institute for Occupational Safety and Health n.d.). Ben was impressed with the thoroughness of the coverage of QWL within the survey. The 41-item survey covered many job-level issues, including workload, participation, resource adequacy, supervisory behavior, promotions, job variety, teamwork, role clarity, and stress management. Cultural issues, including safety climate, harassment and management relations, and physical and mental health outcomes, were covered.

Most importantly to Ben, job satisfaction was also included among the other outcomes measured on the GSS, which also included performance, job commitment, and intentions to leave, with hours of work also addressed. Ben felt confident that he had found a suitable questionnaire to address job satisfaction and employee morale. Ben sent the link for the questionnaire to Lisa. Ben stuck two post-it notes to his computer monitor: one to remind himself to follow-up with Lisa and the other to prompt him to modify his approach to the next set of YERs by finding out what his employees value in their jobs and using that information to gain goal commitments.

CHAPTER 11

The Cultural Conundrum

It was 8:22 a.m., and Ben was extremely frustrated. He had traveled to Latin America to meet a major client. His mission was to learn more about the important consumer market there and to get a better gauge on the customer base in the region. Aside from gathering data through market research, Ben thought it would be helpful to connect with the sales division and meet up with some of the region's largest customers directly. This was his first customer meeting, and as he looked down at his watch for the umpteenth time, he noticed that the sales manager sitting next to him looked totally relaxed. Ramon was a local in the region and had been an extremely successful sales manager through the years. Most importantly, he had a very solid understanding of the market, and he had great relationships with his region's major customers. He liked to be in the field, not giving orders behind a desk. Ben was exasperated, and he wondered how Ramon could be so relaxed. The customer was over 20 minutes late.

"Do you think we should call him?" Ben asked.

"Call him? Why?" Ramon said with a chuckle.

"Well, he's almost thirty minutes late. Maybe he's a no-show," Ben said, failing to hide the irritation in his voice.

"Don't worry, sir. He'll be here!" While Ben didn't share the manager's confidence, he decided to trust him. After all, Ramon understood his local customers. Sure enough, five minutes later, in walked the client. Ben introduced himself, and they all moved into the back office. Ben couldn't believe that the customer didn't apologize, despite being almost 30 minutes late.

The men sat down, and Ramon asked the customer how his family was doing. Ben listened for a few minutes as the two men spoke about their family life and activities. Finally, after losing his patience, Ben interjected with a question about the customer's business. The customer looked at Ben with a mark of irritation on his face. He answered the question, but as the conversation progressed, he disclosed less information than Ben had hoped for. In the end, Ben felt that it was a highly unsuccessful meeting. He was also disappointed with Ramon, thinking he had a good relationship with the client. If that had been the case, Ben felt they would have been able to get more information out of the meeting. Nonetheless, the client seemed cold and even antagonistic throughout the whole discussion. At the end of the day, Ben sat in his hotel room and tried to reflect on what happened during their discussion. He even considered telling Ramon's vice president about his experience. However, he decided to wait and see how the next day's meeting went before mentioning anything.

The following day they were planning to meet with two customers. In both cases, the same thing happened. Ben was beside himself. At the end of the day, he asked Ramon why he didn't have better relationships with his clients. Ramon replied that he did, but that Ben's intrusions during the conversation reflected the fact that he didn't understand the local culture. He explained to Ben that it is often customary to open with a long, personal discussion about family, football (soccer), or other topics unrelated to business. Only after this could one get to the business discussion. He explained that this initial conversation could sometimes last 30 minutes or more and was an important part of relationship building with his customers. When Ben interrupted and delved right into business, he likely offended the customers.

Ben was taken aback by the inference that he was to blame. How could it be his fault? After all, the customers had already wasted time by showing up so late. Didn't they have a business to run? Ben was dumbfounded but decided to go back to his hotel and reevaluate the meetings. The more he thought about it, the more he realized that Ramon may have been right. The customers, despite their tardiness, seemed relaxed and happy to talk with Ramon. However, when Ben started talking business, their whole demeanor had changed. Ben realized that he would have to change his behavior. Through experience, Ben was learning the hard way about cultural bias and framing. As in Ben's case, these concepts are often learned the hard way in virtual teams, or sometimes not at all.

If we examine Ben's experience, there are a few important points that can be learned. The first of these is that despite his extensive travels, Ben didn't have much experience working in Latin America. Therefore, Ben was psychologically framing the experience through his perspective of his upbringing in the United States and specifically the monochronic values of his culture. While Ben comes from a culture that values focusing on a single, linear task at a time and specifically merits punctuality as important, Latin American culture is often very polychronic. Polychronic cultures value relationships over time. Since time is a part of the natural way of life and can therefore be influenced by spontaneity, scheduling precision is less important (Duranti and Di Prata 2009). While Ben had arrived 10 minutes early and was expecting a prompt and timely meeting, the customer was perfectly comfortable arriving later than the agreed-upon time. For Ben, this became a stressful situation in which he actually began to wonder if the customer would show up at all. His local sales manager, however, was perfectly comfortable; and while he didn't mention it, he would have likely shown up just a few minutes before the customer. Furthermore, as the meeting started so late, and Ben was already stressed by this fact, he felt a greater urgency to begin the business discussion as soon as possible to make up for his perception of lost time. This, in turn, offended the customer, who felt that a discussion of relationships and matters that Ben perceived as trivial was as important as the business itself.

Polychronic cultures value relationships over time; as time is a part of the natural way of life and can therefore be influenced by spontaneity, scheduling precision is less important.

Cultural differences are common when businesses expand their activities across global borders. Cultural diversity happens when at least two people with differing demographics come together (McGrath, Berdahl, and Arrow 1995). Given the global nature of the environment, it can be a very important factor in virtual teams. As was stated in earlier chapters, one of the great benefits of having a virtual team is the ability to source unique talent in regions that were not previously accessible. By doing this, organizations increase their level of diversity, creativity, and, in some cases, access to new markets. While there are many benefits to cultural diversity, it is not always without its challenges.

As Ben discovered, the simple perception of time can sometimes translate into serious problems. Yet, this seemingly simple disconnect can sometimes grow into a serious problem. Reverting back to Ben's team, imagine a situation where one employee sets a meeting for 3:00 p.m. However, his international colleague comes from a polychronic culture and calls into the meeting a few minutes late. The person from the monochronic society who set the meeting is furious because, he allowed for exactly 30 minutes to discuss any issues before his next call began at 4:00 p.m. However, because the colleague called in late, the team has only 24 minutes to cover all the material. The organizer proceeds to berate the late caller in front of his peers and expresses his disdain for such lackadaisical and unprofessional work behaviors. On the other hand, the individual who called in late doesn't really understand why his coworker is making such a big deal about it. In his experience, people sometimes call in to a meeting 10 to 15 minutes late and no one says anything. As far as he is concerned, he was right on time! As a result of this single situation, the relationship between the coworkers was tarnished and the resulting fallout could ultimately impact the team as a whole.

Aside from perceptions of time, other considerations of cultural diversity are identified in Geert Hofstede's six dimensions of national culture. These include the Power Distance Index (PDI), individualism versus collectivism (IDV), masculinity versus femininity (MAS), the uncertainty avoidance index (UAI), long-term orientation versus short-term normative orientation (LTO), and indulgence versus restraint (IND) (Hofstede n.d.). For example, the PDI addresses how subordinate employees perceive power or hierarchy as it relates to their superiors. Ben comes from the United States, which is relatively low on the PDI scale. This means that Ben's general perception of power is that it should be equally and justly distributed. However, Ramon, the sales manager whom he met with in Latin America, comes from a country with a fairly high power index. This means that his perception of power is more hierarchal in nature, and thus his perception of superior authority is likely greater than that of Ben's (Clearly Cultural n.d.).

Similarly, the United States has a relatively high IDV as compared to most Latin American countries. This means that Ben's societal perspective is likely more focused on individual needs and abilities. Ben, from the United States, is more likely to rely on his own abilities to get ahead and may therefore be less concerned with the advancement of other colleagues or members of his society. Ramon, on the other hand, would likely perceive the collective society as a more important factor than his own individual advancement. Therefore, as an example, he might be more apt to help a coworker or friend advance than would Ben, even if it came at his own expense. While Hofstede's model is useful in gauging different country cultures, the question still remains: How can Ben and managers like him alleviate some of the difficulties that can come with cultural variance?

To begin with, one way a person can better understand different cultures is to reframe his or her mind. Our brain makes order out of confusion through framing, and thus creates bias based on our own cognitive perceptions. In essence, we judge individuals and situations through the goggles of our own "framed" experiences and that becomes our reality (Shpancer 2010). Recalling the case of the late meeting attendee, imagine the outcome if the meeting organizer were more understanding of the late attendee's culture. Instead of reacting in an inflammatory way, he could have simply called the attendee at a later time and explained that tardiness is not an acceptable behavior in the current organization and to please make sure to be on time moving forward. Such a response would demonstrate empathy and potentially defuse what became a hostile situation.

> *Our brain makes order out of confusion through framing, and thus creates bias based on our own cognitive perceptions. In essence, we judge individuals and situations through the goggles of our own "framed" experiences and that becomes our reality.*

Oftentimes, people are quick to judge others' behaviors without considering the cultural context. This is a very real challenge in the virtual environment. On the other hand, the results can be tremendous when a team figures out how to effectively work through their cultural differences and engage in a productive relationship. Imagine the creative potential of a team where one person calls in from Kansas City, while others call in from Lima, Lagos, Rome, and Oslo! Each member of the team brings with them a wealth of unique experiences, not only culturally, but also potentially from different businesses and industries. Research supports the notion that global and cultural diversity, when aligned with team goals, can be a massive benefit for virtual teams. In a study that examined the possible benefits of diversity in short-term projects, the results showed that heterogeneous teams, or those without any type of language, cultural, geographical diversity, actually had more conflict in their teams and were less cohesive and satisfied with their group than were the culturally diverse group in the tasks they were given (Staples and Zhao 2006).

While culture is often thought of as being defined by the behaviors, values, and norms that people develop in society, other aspects of culture come to play in virtual teams (Groeschl and Doherty 2000). For example, each organization has a unique culture and even a manager can instill a distinct culture in his or her team. Even so, regional differences can have a powerful impact on overall team behavior (Kirkman, Gibson, and Shapiro 2001). Therefore, to facilitate active and progressive communication, a leader and his or her team should work hard to learn about and understand the differences between varying cultures represented on the team. This can help lessen the potential negative impact of working on a team where cultural diversity exists (Robey, Khoo, and Powers 1999).

Research supports the notion that global and cultural diversity, when aligned with team goals, can be a massive benefit for virtual teams.

When conflicts due to cultural differences do occur, it is important for a virtual leader to act in a controlled and collected manner. Having constant flare-ups between team members is not only unproductive, but could even derail the entire project. Virtual leaders must understand that while the communication process is a notable concern for them and their team, overlooking and ignoring the impact of cultural diversity will not likely contribute to successful outcomes. Instead, virtual managers should help their team understand each other's differences and focus on a common and unified goal (Au and Marks 2012). For example, to tell employees from a monochronic society that they are simply "wrong" in their behavior leaves the possibility that they will feel insulted or offended. Rather, it would behoove the virtual leader to set boundaries initially and inform the team that timeliness is greatly valued and tardiness will not be tolerated. In this manner, the leader is not singling any individual employee, but rather he or she is simply setting the rules for the team.

Ben learned an important lesson while working with Ramon in Latin America. He realized that by framing his experience with his limited U.S. perspective, he may have sabotaged his own productivity in his planned research project. Furthermore, if their discussion had been a negotiation or sales call, he might not even have progressed beyond the first meeting. Ben decided that he would try to be more culturally sensitive moving forward. He even thought that this decision was somewhat in line with his commitment to be more empathetic and develop his skills in emotional intelligence. Ben rubbed his head and stared at the floor for a moment, as a startling fact hit him. He still had a heck of a lot to learn. Just then his phone vibrated, and he looked at the screen. The e-mail was from EMEA HR. It seems that another employee had complained about Thomas's belligerent attitude and unwillingness to work with the Dutch team.

Ben had put this problem off for almost a year, and now it was clearly coming to a head. He called his administrative assistant and asked her to book a trip to Amsterdam. Ben felt like he was getting smacked in the face with one challenge after another. His corporate training programs were doing little to alleviate his problems. The lack of sleep from late night and early morning calls was taking their toll, and his wife wasn't pleased about the fact that he often missed dinner to take calls from Asia. Now he had to miss his son's big soccer game to travel to Amsterdam to read Thomas the riot act. The thought of firing him even crossed his mind, but he knew that it wasn't an easy decision, especially in Europe, where it wasn't so easy to let someone go. Ben was exhausted. Regardless, in a week he would be on the plane, and things were going to get a whole lot worse before they got better.

CHAPTER 12

The Lonely, Dark Halls of Isolation

Ben was sitting at his desk and reading a disturbing report. A few members of his team had complained that they felt demotivated and disconnected from the team. Ben wasn't sure who the team members were, but he sure wanted to find out. He tried to keep everyone in the loop. He felt that he had done a good job of managing his team, and he had implemented many new ideas. For example, he set up a team web forum, where everyone could communicate what they were working on, what phase of their project they were in, and other relevant work-related tasks. Ben had frequent calls with his team on both a group and individual level. He had even traveled more in the last year to visit his remote team members than ever before. However, it appeared, based on the report, that it wasn't enough. He was perplexed. What more could he do to motivate his team?

Managers like Ben face many challenges throughout their career. As mentioned, some challenges can be exacerbated while working virtually. While many struggle with these issues, each leader handles these situations in different ways. Some might allow stress to build up until they explode on a team member. Others are proactive in managing the challenges and face them with the best attitude possible, while some others might simply crumble under the pressure. Ben was falling into the former category. The pressure of his new job, new deliverables, a new team, and the added stresses of virtual and international work were proving to be overwhelming. Ben was reaching a tipping point. However, to help alleviate the stress, Ben decided to work on new solutions that might help. He looked into the place he was most comfortable: his work.

In the world of sales and marketing, it is important to bring value to one's customer. In order to differentiate itself from competitors, a firm must bring something to the table that will make it more relevant than its competitors to the customer market it serves. Ben began to think about how this could apply to his team-level management. According to an article in the *Harvard Business Review*, a company can best stay relevant when it continues learning. This helps the organization and its employees remain adaptable and facilitates the ability to react to changes in the marketplace (Wadors 2016). Ben was certainly learning a lot. However, he realized that a big part of his role was to coach his team to success. This was an area where he felt he could really learn more and improve. The problem was that Ben was unwittingly dealing with some of the deeply rooted psychological challenges of team members working remotely.

One of the big problems in virtual work is that doing one's job remotely can feel isolating. Employees call into their team meetings, sometimes with cameras activated and live video feed, and other times not. Virtual employees can spend a lot of time staring at their screen and looking at names of people in their meeting, or slides from the moderator. Oftentimes, this world feels sterile, uninviting, and lacking any personal touch. This can make people feel isolated, and this isolation can create many challenges for otherwise solid employees. Some simply miss the interaction with others in their team. They can get depressed or lose motivation due to the inability to develop relationships with their team members, and these things can lead to a diminished team spirit (Bailey 2013). As a result of limited face-to-face interactions, people who work virtually can feel insulated and alone, which creates greater difficulty for the remote worker (Kirkman et al. 2002).

Working digitally can also create task interdependence, which is the level to which an employee requires input, data, information, and collaborative support to do their job (Van der Vegt, Van de Vliert, and Oosterhof 2003). Depending on the work, the level of task interdependence can vary. However, workers who are in the virtual spectrum often have to sift through an endless void of e-mails, calls, conferences, and tedious files and paperwork. Their share of time with others can often be limited, at best. This social isolation can have implications for the worker and his or her team. When people feel alone in their work, or are isolated socially, this can impact their satisfaction with what they are doing (Maslach and Jackson 1981). Therefore, a manager's role in this environment must be not only to motivate employees, but also to utilize the right tools to alleviate some of the isolation for remote team members. For example, in an effort to enhance the social environment in a team, a manager could incorporate more video technology, where possible.

Additionally, the manager could support team members through online social networks, such as through congratulating a job well done in front of the whole team in a social forum (Wool 2017). This idea hit Ben when he had a team meeting one Friday afternoon. Ben had called in with video conferencing, and most of his team connected with audio only. Ben was leading the meeting and staring at his slides while speaking about the topic at hand. He would solicit feedback from his team during this call, and yet only a few would ever speak. He stared at the names and the little images of microphones, waiting for them to light up and indicate that others were going to speak. At one point, Ben made a joke and was met with utter silence on the call. He began to wonder if his people were even present, so he started to call individuals by name. They always responded in this case, but would then disappear back into silence. Ben knew that if he was frustrated by this, then others in his team might also be impacted. Therefore, he decided to implement a new rule. He required that his team call in through video; no excuses. Once he did this, the team became far more engaged in the calls. In turn, Ben felt more like a facilitator than a lecturer in the meetings, and for him, this was a great change.

When Ben began to think of the social networking piece, he realized that there was room for improvement there too. Currently, the organization had a website where anyone could talk about their projects, but it was really meant for business-related topics only, and not everyone used it. Ben began to think that maybe the team forum might be a terrific way to build team comradery and companionship. He thought that they could make the web forum more personal and include special employee life-events, like birthdays, marriages, births, etc. In this way, team members could learn more about each other than what phase of the project each had completed. Perhaps, he thought, this could help sideline some of the dehumanizing aspects of virtual working for his team. Even the added use of emoticons, such as happy faces, can activate emotional response in the same human brain pathways as nonverbal communication (Yuasa, Saito, and Mukawa 2011).

Furthermore, the social aspect of a team can have great importance for many other factors as well. As mentioned earlier, working in a virtual setting can require a great degree of personal motivation, as a manager is not constantly overseeing each detail of an employee's daily tasks. However, the social network of a virtual team might increase social burden and drive individual team members to increased performance. Research has demonstrated that pressure in a social setting can contribute to increased individual motivation and enhanced commitment toward the team as a whole (Staples and Webster 2007). Along with these challenges, managers can have a difficult time finding ways to truly measure the level of engagement of their team members. A good manager can help facilitate engagement by creating specific agreements for the team, implementing a schedule to highlight team members, instituting clear guidelines for team communication, and educating themselves on the natural developmental stages of team formulation (Evans 2011). Other ways managers can help create greater social bonds would include contacting team members more frequently, providing opportunities for virtual team members to join company events, and even increasing the potential for customer or stakeholder meetings to diminish the feelings of social isolation (Kirkman, Rosen, Gibson, Tesluk and McPherson 2002).

Even the added use of emoticons, such as happy faces, can activate emotional response in the same human brain pathways as nonverbal communication.

Ben spent many hours thinking about how he could implement his new discoveries to build better emotional and social bonds with his team. Along with setting new guidelines for meetings, he decided to especially reach out to those team members who were disconnected from other members of the project. He would set up weekly calls when possible and take a few more minutes to enhance his discussions to move beyond business topics. Ben thought about how often he had called his team and asked "how are things?" before moving on without acknowledging or even really giving them time to answer. This must change, he thought.

Furthermore, he would try to build team cohesiveness through increased team-building exercises when the group was together. He also realized that he rarely contacted some of his team members, simply because they were not managing key components of his current project. He decided to implement changes in this area, too. Ben started to use his own rule of thinking from the customer point of view and adapt it to his team point of view. This helped him visualize the depth of some of the issues many of his team members might be facing. This visualization also motivated him to bring greater relevance as a leader to his team members.

After only a month of implementing some of these basic changes, Ben began to see real results. Meetings were far more productive and engaging, his team seemed more engaged and responsive, and he felt that he was developing better relationships with his team. While happy with the results so far, he knew that it would be very easy to fall into old habits. Therefore, he committed himself to continue with his plan and hopefully become a better leader in the process.

A good manager can help facilitate engagement by creating specific agreements for the team, implementing a schedule to highlight team members, instituting clear guidelines for team communication, and educating themselves on the natural developmental stages of team formulation.

CHAPTER 13

An Additional Perspective

Ben, like many managers, strives to find ways to improve himself through reading and personal research. Researchers try to help managers find better approaches to managing in the potential minefield that is virtual leadership. In a study we conducted, a research project was executed in one of the world's largest consumer goods organizations (Brady 2014). The study aimed to examine the world of virtual working teams within this organization, while specifically examining the impact of factors including the psychological contract and job satisfaction and perceived productivity.

The study involved both qualitative and quantitative research methods, which provided rich insight into the challenges the managers were facing within the company. Several senior-level managers (vice president and director levels) were interviewed, and the data were collected and broken down through content analysis to formulate a case study. From this analysis, a Likert-scale survey was created and sent out to their virtual work teams abroad. These results were then analyzed statistically. The insight gained from the research was meant to help managers like Ben become better leaders and gain insights for overcoming some of the major virtual leadership challenges.

While our study examined perceptions of employees in only one organization, the company is massive and global in scope. At the time of the research, the senior leadership team worked out of the corporate European offices in Switzerland, while the global virtual teams were based in the United States and South America. As in the case of Ben and many real-world managers like him, the leadership team in the study used technology as an enabler to enhance their business functionality and communication abroad. Several managers also iterated the importance of investing in the proper technology to enhance communication effectiveness. Beyond the technology piece, the issue of trust was also a hot topic for these managers.

In general, the managers stated that trust was more than important; it was a necessity. This meant two-way trust for both the team and their leaders. Many said that they *had* to trust their team, or nothing would work. Trust, it was said, is crucial in a normal team, but in the virtual environment it becomes even more essential. This idea reinforces what was stated in previous chapters about the notion of swift trust, and the necessity of building upon it as the relationship develops. One of the leaders went so far as to say that if he worked in the same office with his team, he would have a lot more detail about projects and related topics to work with. However, because he worked virtually, it was inherently harder to build and gain trust, especially when the relationships were new. These discussions exemplified the extreme difficulty, yet great importance, of establishing and maintaining trust in the virtual work environment.

Trust, it was said, is crucial in a normal team, but in the virtual environment it becomes even more essential.

As far as cultural differences were concerned, most of the managers in the studied company agreed that culture didn't create any major barriers to their work. While they were working with people from three different continents, originating from a myriad of varying cultures, most felt that this diversity in culture helped them become better managers and develop better people managing skills in the long run. Some mentioned that small cultural misunderstandings occasionally occurred, but they felt that their company managed the cultural perspective quite well and that their teams worked cohesively.

Outside of the cultural realm, the idea of team expectations proved to be a significant challenge for some leaders. Several leaders mentioned that according to their experience, they sometimes found it difficult to manage the future career and work expectations of their team. Part of this challenge was the fact that some employees found it difficult to express their expectations, and so time was required before they were revealed. In other cases, it came down to the maturity level of the virtual employee and his or her ability/experience in working within the virtual context. Some managers stated that they had acquired people from other managers, and in some cases found that these people didn't work well in the virtual environment and had difficulty communicating and managing some tasks. This supports the importance that Ben placed on hiring the right people after Mary left the company. Equipping the team with the right experience may make all the difference when working in the virtual environment.

Of course, as Chapter 5 illustrated, a huge challenge for virtual managers can be the difference in time across dispersed geographic regions. This was reinforced in discussions with the leadership team. Two of the interviewed leaders, in particular, freely expressed their distaste for working across such distances in time and geography. One said that he had no problem working virtually, but it was the time difference that made it horrible. Another said that the challenge began at what was for most the end of the day. That was when it was the start of working hours in the Americas, and he had four hours to catch up on important matters with the team. Others expressed the social and physical impact of these time differences. Some said that time differences impacted sleeping patterns, while others iterated the potential family consequences of regularly working after-hours at home or in the office.

One of the leaders tried to find the positives of working virtually. He stated that at the very least, he had six hours or so of quiet work before everyone in America woke up. This provided him with time to catch up on less pressing issues. Overall, each team leader was clear about the idea that working across such a large difference in time was challenging at best, and potentially damaging to productivity at worst. This challenge remains pervasive not only in the researched organization, but in many global firms who work in this manner. Further exacerbating the difficulty of managing virtually was the problem of lack of role-clarity. One leader said that his role as a director was clear, but the roles across the virtual spectrum often were not. Another iterated that they (the company) were improving in this area, but they still had a long way to go, and they were not unified on what virtual role-clarity was for each individual.

These interviews of real-world directors and senior leaders provided rich insight into some of the great challenges of working in the challenging environment of virtual teams. However, interviews were only a part of the research. We also statistically analyzed data from questionnaires answered by 103 team members who worked for the European leaders in North and

South America. It was this data that helped the authors better understand the unique challenges of virtual work within this organization.

One of the fundamental factors studied was the psychological contract and its impact on job satisfaction, perceived performance, and trust. The data revealed that in this group, when managers made commitments related to the career aspects of their employees, trust was potentially impacted. For instance, when a manager promises a new career opportunity to an employee and delivers on that promise, trust with his or her employee would likely increase. Recall the story of Ben and Mary. Ben had promised Mary a new career opportunity that, while small, could have helped her develop and enhance her experience and future career opportunities. If Ben had followed through on his word, Mary likely would have trusted him more and he could have built a better relationship with her on the team. Instead, she became dissatisfied and ultimately left the company.

Another compelling conclusion from our study of virtual employees was that role-clarity had a positive impact on job satisfaction. For instance, when their job roles were clear, they were happier about what they were doing. This parallels what was mentioned about role-clarity in Chapter 2. The study also found that in this cohort, greater job satisfaction could increase levels of perceived productivity. So, after considering some outcomes of our study, the real question is what does it really tell us, and how can it help virtual managers?

The quantitative sample cohort was quite small considering that the organization studied has over 100,000 employees. A sample of 103 remote employees participated from the supply chain division in the Americas. Still, within this small cohort, only 37 percent of the participants agreed that their managers had fulfilled their career promises, and a mere 28 percent agreed that the organization had fulfilled its obligations related to promotions. Another interesting note was that 55 percent of the employees felt that it was important for a manager to allow open access to his or her virtual team. Furthermore, 92 percent of the respondents felt that role-clarity had a positive impact on their performance.

These data points, while small, tell a story. The study's data seem to support many of the factors mentioned throughout this book and are presented as reinforcement for important points. Virtual managers such as Ben have a lot on their plate at any given time. Sometimes too much information can provide a data dump that results in stagnate action. However, our study illustrates the importance of some key factors including trust, role-clarity, and job satisfaction. Some of the outcomes could be seen as somewhat alarming, such as the number of people who felt that the organization and management were actually fulfilling their promises related to career fulfillment. As mentioned earlier, situations like this could cause employees to feel that they have no future in the company. Managers should be attentive to these indicators. Employee perceptions can be gathered either by the company or by third parties to determine if target satisfaction metrics are actually being met. This information can provide important insight for virtual managers.

Throughout the course of their day, virtual team managers must manage many tasks and handle many issues. They must also make many decisions that can have critical effects on business activity, the company, and their employees. Employee satisfaction data can clarify important points that can help remote team managers make better decisions. The psychological contract has been mentioned throughout this book. The key takeaway from our research is the idea that promises managers make, even in passing, can have potential impact on trust and manager/employee relationships moving forward. This is especially true when the implied promise has a career-related focus. Therefore, virtual managers need to be extremely careful about promises or commitments they make to their employees. They also need to be very certain that their team members have clearly defined job roles and that they understand their responsibilities. Essentially, managers must watch what they say and write, as even small comments could be perceived by employees as commitments.

In the next chapter, we will summarize what we have covered in this book and will consider a model that will help virtual leaders find the right path on the road to building an effective team.

Essentially, managers must watch what they say and/or write, as even small comments could be perceived by employees as commitments.

CHAPTER 14

That's a Wrap

Ben's phone rang at exactly 10:00 a.m. Ben's boss, Lisa, the vice president of his division, was on the line. She had called to inform him that she was very happy with his performance and that she would be increasing his salary and stock options in the coming year. She specifically noted that his team's 360-degree reviews had improved remarkably in the last six months.

Ben couldn't believe that he had already been in his new role for over a year. As he looked back, he realized he had made many mistakes. Even so, he tried to use each one as an opportunity to grow and improve. Overall, it seemed to be working. His biggest regret was losing one of his star employees, Mary. He knew that his actions, or inaction, were the primary reason for her resignation. In hindsight, if he had just kept his word and given her the leadership opportunity she wanted, she might still have been the shining star on his European team. Nonetheless, it was a lesson learned and a hard one at that. Additionally, Ben thought about how culturally naïve he had been while meeting his sales team's important customers in Latin America. If he had been more prepared and had done just a little more research, he could have made that trip much more productive and worthwhile from a research perspective. Instead, his sales manager had to suffer through awkward conversations and probably later apologize for Ben's seemingly rude behavior.

Ben had taken this job feeling rather confident in his abilities to lead his team through the virtual communication environment. He felt that his past experience had fully equipped him for the challenges that would lie ahead. Instead, he repeatedly stumbled and, through luck and personal growth, developed his skill set in this area. Still, he knew that mistakes happen. They are part of the learning process. However, he felt that he handled things well and, most importantly, he continued to develop his leadership skills and had improved. Ben knew that looking forward, he would have additional challenges and opportunities to grow.

Throughout the book, we have used Ben's case study to illustrate several important examples of challenges that real managers face in the virtual leadership realm. While Ben is a fictional character, the trials he goes through are based on real-life stories and lessons learned by actual virtual managers. Academic theory is not always congruent with practical application. Therefore, it is important to use management theory and research to create practical, real-world applications. The aim is for managers of organizational virtual teams (VTs) to use Ben's case study as a basis for improving their own awareness and capabilities.

The following simple model will hopefully help managers to increase their abilities and potential success as virtual leaders. People who work in the virtual environment are often inundated with sounds. Alarms, beeps, bells, notifications, rings, and other sounds all tug at a manager's ear, crying for attention. This myriad of sounds gave rise to the name for our model. The BEEP-THEM model summarizes the key ideas of this book in an easy-to-remember format:

B-*uild trust*
E-*mpower*
E-*motional intelligence*
P-*romises and the psychological contract*
T-*hink multiculturally*
H-*ire the right people*
E-*nergize the team*
M-*ake time to sleep and live*

The first B—Build Trust

As Chapter 4 illustrated, trust is an essential building block to creating a truly functional VT. However, trust doesn't come easy, and it can dissipate all too quickly. A virtual leader must work hard to initiate and consistently build trust between himself or herself and the team. As an important part of this, managers must follow through on both work and verbal commitments in a timely manner. It also can be useful to explain to the team the importance of following through on commitments and obligations. Once trust is established, VT leaders need to make sure to manage it and develop it into a solid base for their team.

The Mighty E—Empower

As earlier chapters in this book clearly delineated, one of the great potential benefits of VTs is the fact that a manager can search out unique talent across the globe. No longer must companies hire only within the proverbial fishbowl of their local geographic area. Rather, the diffusion of technology has opened up a vast ocean of opportunities to seek out diverse individuals who think differently and have unique skill sets. Why wouldn't a VT manager use this to his or her advantage? It's not about delegating jobs; delegation is just giving someone something to do so a manager doesn't have to do it. Empowerment, on the other hand, is affording people the responsibility of using their special talents or abilities creatively to develop themselves as leaders and enhance the capabilities of their colleagues. In earlier chapters, we considered the potential benefits of employee empowerment using the case of Ben, as well as other studies. An important point to remember is that VT managers have access to a swath of great talent, and to let that go unused would be a terrible waste. Empower your team and watch it grow.

> *Empowerment, on the other hand, is affording people the responsibility of using their special talents or abilities creatively to develop themselves as leaders and enhance the capabilities of their colleagues.*

E^2—Emotional Intelligence

Humans are emotional beings. Leaders who have the ability to read and respond to these emotions could greatly improve their capabilities as managers. While empathy and appreciation of the emotional situations and stresses of others are important for any manager, having a high emotional intelligence, or emotional quotient, is critical for VT managers. Communicating through wires and the cloud is all well and good. However, it's easy for people to get lost behind their screens, which can foster isolation and disenchantment. When managers can understand their employees' emotional states, they can be more responsive in helping and resolving problems. By doing this, they can become better coaches, building up their team one person at a time.

P—The Power of a Promise
and the Psychological Contract

As Chapter 8 illustrated, a casual promise can have strong implications down the road. For example, a simple, "Hey, if you keep doing so well, I'll have to give you a promotion," might seem innocuous in a casual conversation. However, to the receiver of those words, the statement could be perceived as a real commitment and expectation. We considered the importance of the psychological contract and the implications of violating it. Whatever such expectations are called, managers should, as much as is possible, be certain to follow through on commitments made to their teams. This is especially true in the virtual realm, where verbal communication is often minimized and even casual commitments could potentially be amplified.

> *Whatever such expectations are called, managers should always be certain to follow through on commitments to their teams.*

T—Think Multiculturally

One of the great things about VTs is that for any organization or manager, they can provide the opportunity to mine talent from virtually anywhere on earth. Hiring a global assortment of talented performers can enrich the company and its culture and might even increase efficiencies in the long term. Multicultural teams can provide unique and different perspectives and solutions and can contribute to better understanding of local markets in international settings. Of course, multicultural teams can also provide opportunities for misunderstandings and culturally related conflict. Even the simplest gesture could be misconstrued and considered offensive. Therefore, it behooves a VT leader to take the time to learn about his or her team members' cultures. This does not imply that a VT manager must conduct a comprehensive study of each represented culture under his or her wing (although that would be interesting and probably very beneficial). However, even taking a few minutes to learn some of the important aspects of each culture and market could provide great opportunities for building better relationships and decreasing misunderstandings. As in the story of Ben in Latin America, various aspects of business are viewed differently among cultures. Managers who work with people from cultures that value relationships over time would do well to understand the driving forces behind this type of behavior. This is not to say that a VT manager should accept that a person is late all of the time because of his or her culture. However, cultural understanding could mean that a manager might better respond with empathy and relatability. The goal of a good team is to progress and move forward with efficiency. Being more sympathetic of others and their cultures is at a minimum a great way to start, and it could be instrumental in forging solid relationships with team members.

One final note on culture for native English-speaking managers: watch what you say, especially when using humor and sarcasm. It is common for some members of U.S. and British societies to use sarcasm in a humorous tone to make a joke, or simply to lighten a situation. However, it is important to understand that for some nonnative English speakers, humor and sarcasm can be psychologically decoded incorrectly. Therefore, the resulting message can be misunderstood, confusing, or even offensive. While this, of course, is not the intention of the native speaker, it should be a consideration, especially when communicating with employees for whom English is not the first language.

Being more sympathetic of others and their culture is at a minimum a great way to start, and beyond that it could be instrumental in forging solid relationships with team members from other cultures.

H—Hire the Right People

If a good hire in a traditional team is worth its weight in gold, then a good hire in the virtual setting is like discovering the source of gold. As we saw in Chapter 9, a VT manager is only as good as his or her people, and a bad hire can be a bad career move. Think about some of the general things that a manager relies on remote employees to do effectively. They have to execute their tasks in a timely manner, work with other cross-functional team members across the globe to deliver executables, efficiently manage their work portfolio, while at the same time maintaining proper communication with relevant stakeholders, assist their manager in any deliverables that they may require to execute on, manage their budget, and attend and participate in any organizational trainings and meetings. Ideally, remote workers should execute all these tasks, along with any others that may be required, with a positive attitude. In the virtual world, the manager has less direct face-to-face contact with new hires, so swift trust becomes necessary from the initiation of the relationship as well.

When the wrong person is hired, all of the above can quickly go out the window and this can increase stress for a VT manager. As if VT managers didn't have enough stress in the first place, bad hires have the potential to compound stress and make life a virtual hell for all involved. Beyond becoming proficient in the interview process, what can managers do to make sure they hire the right people from the beginning for their remote team?

1. Engage in behavioral interviews and utilize effective personality tests to better gauge candidates (Ferrazzi n.d.).
2. Look for people who have the right skills. They are self-sufficient, punctual, and organized; have a strong technical inclination; value results; and are effective problem solvers (Young Entrepreneur Council 2018).
3. Seek out people who are culturally aware and have a high propensity for reliable communication.
4. Ask the right open-ended questions, and seek to understand if candidates have the right experience to work in a remote environment.

Of course, hiring is just the beginning. Of equal importance is the process of onboarding a new hire. As was illustrated in the chapter on job satisfaction, it's good to have satisfied people working for the team. However, when someone is hired, dropped into the position, given no direction whatsoever, and told to do the job, happiness and effectiveness may end up being a mere fleeting thought. Therefore, virtual managers must make sure that new hires on their team have the following items, along with their HR package of rules, regulations, and expense management files:

1. Direction or, more specifically, role-clarity. Chapter 3 clearly illustrated the importance of role-clarity in remote teams. For new hires, role-clarity may not come easy, especially if they work for a matrix-type organization. Virtual leaders should work hard to specify clear key performance indicators (KPIs) that are major requirements of the job. Furthermore, they should clarify specific roles within the team itself. Having this knowledge hopefully would help fledgling team members fly more quickly and start being productive.

2. Inspiration. In the virtual environment, it's likely that new employees will have limited time with their managers, so it is wholly important that during the time they do have in direct communication with them, managers should try to inspire them and be available to them for any initial questions or issues.

3. Internal marketing. It doesn't take years of academic research to come to the conclusion that people who love their companies probably enjoy their jobs. A company, or a brand, can be the catalyst, not only for consumers to buy, but for employees to get excited about the organization they work for. When people feel connected to something, they may put forth more effort and work harder. Since a virtual manager is the most likely company connection for a remote employee, with just a little marketing effort, a leader can instill excitement about the company and/or the brand. As a result, new hires can come to feel a part of something much bigger than themselves.

E—Energize the Team

Working remotely can be, well, lonely. That's why it is so important to engage the team and give them the energy and desire to keep on going. Managers are the gateway to the company for their remote teams.

They also need to be the cheerleaders, motivators, and energizers of their people. This can be difficult when leaders never see their people and communicate primarily through texts, e-mails, and online forums. Nevertheless, it can be done.

One way to energize people on a VT is to give them relevant responsibilities that bring value to the group and their careers. Another way remote managers can help their people stay energized is to keep them connected. Managers can do this by checking in regularly, scheduling one-on-one meetings, and making themselves available to their team. Quick and dependable responses might also help the team stay connected. Distance working is hard, but it can be a bigger challenge when the manager is never available or ignores texts and calls. Of course, time is a factor, and many VT managers have limited time to reach out to each and every employee. However, regularly scheduled staff meetings can help in this area. Additionally, a manager might consider assigning an individual on the team the task of keeping connected with the rest of the team. This person, preferably someone with high leadership potential, could act as the liaison between the manager and the rest of the team. Creating an online webpage where the team can keep in contact throughout the life of the project can also help. Keeping the team excited may be challenging, but it doesn't have to be impossible.

M—Make Time to Sleep and Live

This step may seem counterintuitive in a business book, but it is hugely important for a virtual manager. VT leaders work in an environment where time never stops. It may be 6:00 or 7:00 in the evening where they live, but their teams in Asia are just getting the workday started. A European VT manager may be planning a nice dinner with his or her family, but the individual needs to take yet another call in order to speak with a U.S. employee who is just starting the workday. In our research study, most of the vice presidents and directors who were leading VTs agreed that sleep was a challenge and did not come easy. Some said working virtually definitely impacted their family time in the evenings.

Many virtual leaders would work 24/7, if it were possible, but it's not. People are not robots, and there are consequences, both long and short term, to missing out on the all-important sleeping hours. If people really want to work better and more efficiently, they really should make sure to sleep more. Lack of sleep can cause mental fog by negatively impacting cognitive processes that affect thinking. It can be linked to depression, increased aging, and forgetting meetings (and everything else), and it can impair judgment (Perri n.d.). Worst than that, not getting enough sleep can lead to increased rates of morbidity and mortality. It has been associated with higher incidences of diabetes, cancer, heart disease, high blood pressure, stroke, and even death (Loria 2018). The list goes on. So, what can a busy manager do?

One thing is for sure, though, if you want to hit your business goals, it's a lot easier to do it if your brain and body are functioning at peak performance.

It's easy to get wrapped up in work, and sometimes, there's no way to avoid late nights, such as during quarter-end or year-end. However, beyond those times, virtual managers should set a schedule for sleep. Between seven and nine hours a day should do. During these times, all phones and devices should be turned off; and even before going to bed, managers should take some time to detox the brain from the blue screens. There are different ways to do this, such as reading, meditating, relaxing, etc. It goes without saying that spending time with family and exercising are also greatly important. However, it's up to each individual manager to find the time and discipline to manage his or her schedule. Just remember, if Richard Branson, Elon Musk, Tim Cook, Bill Gates, Mark Zuckerberg, and Jack Dorsey, among many others, can find the time for fitness, it's possible that anyone can do it. Sometimes it helps to think that life is about more than KPIs, objectives, and strategy. One thing is for sure, though, if you want to hit your business goals, it's a lot easier to do it if your brain and body are functioning at peak performance. Everybody has heard the old adage, "work smarter, not harder." However, another way to look at it might be: *live better to lead better.*

Conclusion

Ben's eyes were tired and his fingers were tired from typing. It had been a stressful day, but he was happy. Things were finally falling into place for Ben and his team. He had wrapped up another fourth quarter with solid numbers and had accrued positive market share in the face of stiff competition. He knew he couldn't have done it without his team. When Ben began this job almost two years ago, he struggled in some areas. He had worked as a remote team leader before, but he had never had so many people across such a huge swath of the globe. Nonetheless, he worked hard throughout the year, learned from his mistakes, and set himself up for a better future. Ben felt connected with his team, and overall he and his team had high level of trust for each other. While he had lost a few good employees, he had filled those voids with solid performers.

In what he felt was his biggest accomplishment, Ben turned the tides with one of his most difficult employees, Thomas. Thomas, it had seemed, was losing motivation and didn't like to work outside of regular hours. However, Ben made the effort to have a one-on-one meeting with him in Amsterdam, and they had an in-depth discussion about Thomas's career expectations, his work desires, and the fact that he felt lost due to lack of role-clarity and multiple line managers. Ben listened empathetically and focused on truly understanding Thomas's position. After all was said and done, Ben sympathized with Thomas, gave him clearly defined KPIs, and limited other managing stakeholders' influence over his role. Furthermore, Ben discovered that Thomas really wanted to progress and grow in the company, so Ben utilized his talent and gave him extra responsibilities as team leader in several key areas, which Thomas took with gratitude, even given the knowledge that he would likely have more work and longer hours. Since that meeting, Thomas had blossomed into a star employee, and had helped Ben's team grow in the areas where he had leadership governance. Ben had experienced so much frustration early on with Thomas, and yet all it took was a two-hour face-to-face meeting and listening with empathy and understanding for Ben to be able to change everything.

Of course, Ben still had areas of improvement to work on, but overall, he was succeeding as a virtual leader. He swore to continue developing himself and learning new ways to improve. For now though, it was Friday night, and Ben was going home to spend some much needed time with his family. He switched off his computer, put his iPad and phone in his bag, and walked away from his desk and into the darkness of the office. He was living the life of a virtual leader, and now he was going to have a great weekend catching up on some much needed sleep.

References

Oxforddictionaries.com. 2018. "Trust." *The Oxford English dictionary (3rd ed.)*. https://en.oxforddictionaries.com/definition/trust

Andrews, P. August, 2004. "Trust-building for A Virtual Team." *IBM Business Consulting*. http://www-935.ibm.com/services/us/imc/pdf/g510-3949-trust-building.pdf

Argyris, C. 1960. *Understanding Organizational Behavior*. Homewood, IL: The Dorsey Press Inc.

Armstrong, M. 2006. *A Handbook of Human Resource Practice*. London, UK: Kogan Page Business Books.

Arnold, J., R. Randall and F. Patterson. 2016. *Work Psychology: Understanding Human Behavior in the Workplace*. 6th ed. London, UK: Pearson.

Asprey, W., and P. E. Cerruzi. 2008. *The Internet and American Business*. Cambridge, MA: The MIT Press.

Au, Y., and Marks, A. 2012. "Virtual Teams are Literally and Metaphorically Invisible: Forging Identity in Culturally Diverse Virtual Teams." *Employee Relations* 34, no. 3, pp. 270–87. https://www.emeraldinsight.com/doi/abs/10.1108/01425451211217707

Bagley, R. O. March 1, 2013. "How to Hire Successfully: Focus on Mission, Values, Talent." *Forbes*. https://www.forbes.com/sites/rebeccabagley/2013/03/01/how-to-hire-successfully/#7750f2c51749

Bailey, S. March 5, 2013. "How To Beat The Five Killers Of Virtual Working." *Forbes*. https://www.forbes.com/sites/sebastianbailey/2013/03/05/how-to-overcome-the-five-major-disadvantages-of-virtual-working/#57a0b1412734

Barczak, G., F. Lassk, and J. Mulki. November, 2010. "Antecedents of Team Creativity: An Examination of Team Emotional Intelligence, Team Trust and Collaborative Culture." *Creativity and Innovation Management* 19, no. 4, pp. 332–245. https://doi.org/10.1111/j.1467-8691.2010.00574.x

Boule, M. January, 2008. "Best Practices for Working in a Virtual Team Environment." *Library Technology Reports.*

Brady, J. 2014. "Implications of the Psychological Contract on Virtual Team Leadership in a Global Consumer Goods Organization." DBA diss., SBS Swiss Business School, Zurich, Switzerland.

Brandt, V., W. England, and S. Ward. November–December, 2011. "Virtual Teams: As Telecommunications Technology Makes It Possible to Assemble Teams Made Up of Individuals Dispersed across the Globe, It Becomes Essential to Understand How Teams Function Differently When They Don't Meet Face to Face." *Research-Technology Management* 54, no. 6. https://www.questia.com/library/journal/1G1-272739240/virtual-teams-as-telecommunications-technology-makes

Brunetto, Y., S. T. Teo, K. Shacklock, and R. Farr-Wharton. July, 2012. "Emotional Intelligence, Job Satisfaction, Well-Being and Engagement: Explaining Organizational Commitment and Turnover Intentions in Policing." *Human Resource Management Journal* 22, no. 4, pp. 428–41. https://doi.org/10.1111/j.1748-8583.2012.00198.x

Burack, E. H. 1993. *Corporate Resurgence and the New Employment Relationships: After the Reckoning.* Westport, CT: Quorum Books.

Cascio, W. F., and S. Shurygailo. 2003. "E-Leadership and Virtual Teams." *Organizational Dynamics* 31, pp. 362–7. http://dx.doi.org/10.1016/S0090-2616(02)00130-4

Chang, K. T. 2008. "Psychological Contracts and Knowledge Exchange in Virtual Teams." ICIS 2008 Proceedings, Paper 146. http://aisel.aisnet.org/icis2008/146

Cherry, K. October 23, 2018. "What is Democratic Leadership?" *verywellmind.com.* https://www.verywellmind.com/what-is-democratic-leadership-2795315

Chhay, R. V., and B. H. Kleiner. July/August, 2013. "Effective Communication in Virtual Teams." *Industrial Management* 55, no. 4. https://www.questia.com/magazine/1P3-3055519861/effective-communication-in-virtual-teams

Chu, H. C., and C.-Y. Fu. n.d. "An Investigation of Leadership Styles and Psychological Contracts." *ERIC Online submission*, pp. 663–9. https://files.eric.ed.gov/fulltext/ED492423.pdf

Clearly Cultural. n.d. "Clearly Cultural Making Sense of Cross Cultural Communication." http://www.clearlycultural.com/geert-hofstede-cultural-dimensions/power-distance-index, (Accessed September 10, 2018).

CNBC-TV. 2013. "Internet Penetration to Boost Ecommerce Businesses." *moneycontrol.com*.http://www.moneycontrol.com/news/business/internet-penetration-to-boost-ecommerce-businesses-experts_964668.html

Conway, N., and R. B. Briner. March, 2002. "A Daily Diary Study of Affective Responses to Psychological Contract Breach and Exceeded Promises." *Journal of Organizational Behavior* 23, no. 3, pp. 287–302. https://doi.org/10.1002/job.139

Coyle-Shapiro, J., A. M. Jacqueline, and M. Parzefall. 2008. "Psychological Contracts." In: *The SAGE Handbook of Organizational Behavior*, eds. C. L. Cooper and J. Barling. London, UK: Sage, pp. 17–34.

Coyle-Shapiro, J., and L. Kessler. November, 2000. "Consequences of the Psychological Contract for the Employment Relationship: A Large Scale Survey." *Journal of Management Studies* 37, no. 7, pp. 903–30. https://doi.org/10.1111/1467-6486.00210

Coyle-Shapiro, J., A. M. Jacqueline, and I. Kessler. 2002. "Exploring Reciprocity through the Lens of the Psychological Contract: Employee and Employer Perspectives." *European Journal of Work and Organizational Psychology* 11, no. 1, pp. 69–86. http://dx.doi.org/10.1080/13594320143000852

Cutajar, M. September 2, 2017. "Pros & Cons of Team Leadership Styles." *Bizfluent.com*. https://bizfluent.com/info-8117744-pros-cons-team-leadership-styles.html

Davidson, P. 2001. *The Changing Nature of Psychological Contract in the IT Industry*. Research Papers in Human Resource Management. England, UK: Kingston Business School.

Davis, K. E., and M. Todd. January, 1982. "Friendship and Love Relationships." *Advances in Descriptive Psychology* 2, pp. 10–112.

Davis, S. M., and P. R. Lawrence. May 1978. "Problems of Matrix Organizations." *Harvard Business Review*. https://hbr.org/1978/05/problems-of-matrix-organizations

De Jong, J., and R. Schalk, and N. De Cuyper. November, 2009. "Balanced Versus Unbalanced Psychological Contracts in Temporary and Permanent Employment: Associations with Employee Attitudes." *Management and Organization Review* 5, no. 3, pp. 329–51. https://ssrn.com/abstract=1495304 or http://dx.doi.org/10.1111/j.1740-8784.2009.00156.x

De Vos, A., A. Meganck, and D. Buyens. 2006. "The Role of the Psychological Contract in Retention Management: Confronting HR-managers' and Employees' views on Retention Factors' and the Relationship with Employees' Intentions to Stay." Working Paper, Faculty of Economics and Business Administration, Ghent University, Belgium 06/374, Ghent University, Faculty of Economics and Business Administration.

DeLeon, M. May 8, 2015a. "The Importance of Emotional Intelligence at Work." *Entrepreneur.* https://www.entrepreneur.com/article/245755

DeLeon, M. April 9, 2015b. "What Really Happens When You Hire the Wrong Candidate." *Entrepreneur.* https://www.entrepreneur.com/article/244730

Doyle, C. E. 2003. *Work and Organizational Psychology: An Introduction with Attitude.* Hove, England: Psychology Press.

Duranti, G., and O. Di Prata. 2009. "Everything Is About Time: Does It have the Same Meaning All Over the World?" Paper presented at PMI⁻ Global Congress 2009—EMEA, Amsterdam, North Holland, The Netherlands. Newtown Square, PA: Project Management Institute, 2009. https://www.pmi.org/learning/library/everything-time-monochronism-polychronism-orientation-6902

Egelend, B. July 1, 2010. "The Complexity of Virtual Teams." https://pmtips.net/blog-new/complexity-virtual-teams

Espinosa, J. A., and E. Carmel. September, 2004. "The Impact of Time Separation on Coordination in Global Software Teams: A Conceptual Foundation." *Software Process: Improvement and Practice* 8, no. 4. https://doi.org/10.1002/spip.185

Evans, J. April 4, 2011. "8 Tips for Effective Virtual Teams." *Psychology Today.* https://www.psychologytoday.com/us/blog/smartwork/2011 04/8-tips-effective-virtual-teams

Fermin, J. December 6, 2017. "Why Managers MUST Focus on Emotional Intelligence." *Huffington Post*. https://www.huffingtonpost .com/jeff-fermin/why-managers-must-focus-o_b_8547560.html

Ferrazzi, K. March 20, 2012a. "Virtual Teams Can Outperform Traditional Teams." *Harvard Business Review*. http://blogs.hbr.org/ cs/2012/03/how_virtual_teams_can_outperfo.html

Ferrazzi, K. October 8, 2012b. "How to Build Trust in a Virtual Work-place." *Harvard Business Review*. http://blogs.hbr.org/2012/10/ how-to-build-trust-in-virtual

Ferrazzi, K. April 12, 2013. "How to Avoid Virtual Miscommunication." *Harvard Business Review*. http://blogs.hbr.org/2013/04/how-to-avoid-virtual-miscommun

Ferrazzi, K. December, 2014. "Getting Virtual Teams Right." *Harvard Business Review*. https://hbr.org/2014/12/getting-virtual-teams-right

Ferrell, J. Z., and K. C. Herb. 2012. "Improving Communication in Virtual Teams." *Society for Industrial and Organizational Psychology*. http://www.siop.org/WhitePapers/Visibility/VirtualTeams.pdf

Fiske, S. T., and S. E. Taylor. 1991. *Social Cognition*. New York, NY: McGraw-Hill.

Flynn, D. June 17, 2014. "Managing a Team Across 5 Time Zones." *Harvard Business Review*. https://hbr.org/2014/06/managing-a-team-across-5-time-zones

Follet, J. April 27, 2009. "Using Web Software for Collaborative Work on Virtual UX Teams." *uxmatters.com*. http://www.uxmatters.com/ mt/archives/2009/04/using-web-software-for-collaborative-work-on-virtual-ux-teams.php

Foster, D. October 10, 2012. "How to Bring Role Clarity to Your Team." *coach-danfoster.com*. http://www.coachdanfoster.com/2012/10/how-bring-role-clarity-to-your-team

Garrett, A. October 9, 2013. "Crash Course in Managing a Virtual Team." *Management Today*. https://www.managementtoday.co.uk/ crash-course-in-managing-virtual-team/article/735128

Gascoigne, B. n.d. "History of Communication." *HistoryWorld*, from 2001 ongoing. http://www.historyworld.net/wrldhis/PlainTextHistories.asp? groupid=929&HistoryID=aa93&gtrack=pthc

Griffin, R. W., and A. O'Leary-Kelley. 2004. *The Dark Side of Organizational Behavior*. Hoboken, NJ: John Wiley & Sons.

Groeschl, S., and L. Doherty. January, 2000. "Conceptualizing Culture." *Cross Cultural Management* 7, no. 4, pp. 12–17. https://doi.org/10.1108/17410390910993536

Gunduz Cekmecelioglu, H., A. Gunsel, and T. Ulutas. October, 2012. "Effects of Emotional Intelligence on Job Satisfaction: An Empirical Study on Call Center Employees." *Procedia—Social and Behavioral Sciences*, 58, pp. 363–9. https://doi.org/10.1016/j.sbspro.2012.09.1012

Hall, E. T. 2000. *Understanding Cultural Differences, Germans, French and Americans*. Yarmouth, Canada: Intercultural Press.

Harrel, G., and T. Daim. January, 2010. "Virtual Teams and the Importance of Building Trust." *IT Professional* 11, no. 6. https://doi.org/10.1109/MITP.2009.135

Harwood, R. n.d. "The Role of the Psychological Contract in the Contemporary Workplace: An Interview with Prof. Denise M. Rousseau." *rafeharwood.com*. https://rafeharwood.com/articles/psychological-contract, (Accessed October 5th, 2018).

Herriot, P., and C. Pemberton. 1995. *New Deals: The Revolution in Management Careers*. Sussex, UK: John Wiley & Sons.

Herriot, P. 2001. *The Employment Relationship: A Psychological Perspective*. Hove, UK: Psychology Press.

Herzberg, F., B. Mausner, and B. B. Snyderman. 1959. *The Motivation to Work*. New York, NY: John Wiley & Sons.

Hill, S. N., and K. B. Bartol. June 13, 2018. "Five Ways to Improve Communication in Virtual Teams." *MIT Sloan Management Review* Fall 2018.

Hofstede, G. n.d. "National Culture." *Hofstede Insights*. https://www.hofstede-insights.com/models/national-culture, (Accessed September 8, 2018).

Hoppock, R. 1977. *Job Satisfaction,* Reprint Edn. New York, NY: Arno Press.

Iaconna, C. S., and S. Weisband. "Developing trust in virtual teams." *Proceedings of the 30th Hawaii International Conference on Systems Science* 2, no. 5, 412–20. https://dl.acm.org/citation.cfm?id=938573

Issacs, L. March/April, 2012. "Creating Successful Virtual Teams in a New Age." *Information Management* 46, no. 2.

Jackson, P. J., and J. M. V. Wielen. 1998. *Teleworking: International Perspectives: From Telecommuting to the Virtual Organization*. London, UK: Routledge.

Jane, M. n.d. "The Importance of Teamwork in an Organizational Setting." *Small Business—Chron.com*. http://smallbusiness.chron.com/importance-teamwork-organizational-setting-23333.html, (Accessed November 1, 2018).

Jarvenpaa, S. L., and D. E. Leidner. June, 1999. "Communication and Trust in Global Virtual Teams." *Organization Science* 10, no. 6, pp. 791–816. https://doi.org/10.1287/orsc.10.6.791

Johnson, K. 2010. *Virtual Leadership: Required Competencies for Effective Leaders*. Ithaca, NY: Cornell University IRL School: Centre for Advanced Human Resource Studies Cornell University.

Juneja, P. n.d. "Clarity of Roles within a Team." *Management Study Guide (MSG)*. http://managementstudyguide.com/clarity-of-roles-within-a-team.htm, (Accessed 30 September 2018).

Kahai, S. August 9, 2011. "How Important Is It To Manage Temporal Diversity in Virtual Teams?" https://www.leadingvirtually.com/leading-virtual-teams-by-managing-temporal-diversity

Kayworth, T. R., and D. E. Leidner. Winter 2001–2002. "Leadership Effectiveness in Global Virtual Teams." *Journal of Management Information Systems* 18, no. 3, pp. 7–40.

Kirkman, B. L., C. B. Gibson, and D. L. Shapiro. 2001. "Exporting Teams: Enhancing the Implementation and Effectiveness of Work Teams in Global Affiliates." *Organizational Dynamics* 30, no. 1, pp. 12–29. http://dx.doi.org/10.1016/S0090-2616(01)00038-9

Kirkman, B. L., B. Rosen, C. B. Gibson, P. E. Tesluk, and S. O. McPherson. August, 2002. "Five Challenges to Virtual Team Success: Lessons from Sabre, Inc." *The Academy of Management Executive* 16, pp. 67–79. https://doi.org/10.5465/ame.2002.8540322

Kotter, J. P. April, 1973. "The Psychological Contract: Managing the Joining up Process." *Management Review* 15, 91–9. https://doi.org/10.2307/41164442

Landsberger, H. A. 1958. *Hawthorne Revisited—Management and the Worker, its Critics, and Developments in Human Relations in Industry.* Ithica, NY: Cornell University Press.

Lawler, E. E. 1994. *Motivation in Work Organizations*, Reprint Edn. New York, NY: Wiley.

Lee, H.-W., and C.-H. Liu. April, 2009. "The Relationship among Achievement Motivation, Psychological Contract and Work Attitudes", *Social Behavior and Personality: An International Journal* 37, no. 3,p. 321. http://dx.doi.org/10.2224/sbp.2009.37.3.321

Lipnack, J., and J. Stamps. 2000. *Virtual Teams: People Working Across Boundaries with Technology.* New York, NY: John Wiley & Sons, Inc.

Locke, E. A. 1976. "The Nature and Causes of Job Satisfaction." In *Handbook of Industrial and Organizational Psychology,* ed. M. D. Dunnette. Chicago: Rand McNally, IL, pp. 1297–343.

Loria, K. September 3, 2018. "Sleep Deprivation Can Kill You—Here's What Sleeping Less than 7 hours per Night Does to Your Body and Brain." *Business Insider UK.* https://www.businessinsider.com.au/sleep-deprivation-effects-on-your-body-brain-2018-8

Lyons, T. F. 1971. "Role Clarity, Need for Clarity, Satisfaction, Tension, and Withdrawal." *Organizational Behavior & Human Performance,* 6, pp.99–100.http://deepblue.lib.umich.edu/bitstream/handle/2027.42/33731/0000245.pdf;jsessionid=22119037E7C3FFA1D2390687B BF96EA7?sequence=1.

Mackay, J. March 9, 2010. "Creating a High Trust Organization." *John Mackey's Blog.* https://www.wholefoodsmarket.com/blog/john-mackeys-blog/creating-high-trust-organization

Majchzrak, A., and A. Malhotra. 2004. "Enabling Knowledge Creation in Far-flung Teams: Best Practices for IT Support and Knowledge Sharing." *Journal of Knowledge Management,* 8, no. 4, pp. 75–88. https://doi.org/10.1108/13673270410548496

Maslach, C., and S. E. Jackson. April, 1981. "The Measurement of Experienced Burnout." *Journal of Organizational Behavior* 2, no. 2, pp. 99–113. https://doi.org/10.1002/job.4030020205

Maslow, A. H. 1970. *Motivation and Personality,* 2nd ed. New York, NY: Harper & Row.

Mayo, E. 1988. *The Social Problems of an Industrial Civilization,* Reprint Edn. New Hampshire: Ayer Company Publishers.

Maznevski, M. May 1, 1994. "Understanding Our Differences: Performance in Decision-Making Groups with Diverse Members." *Human Relations.* https://doi.org/10.1177%2F001872679404700504

McGrath, J. E., J. L. Berdahl, and H. Arrow. 1995. "Traits, Expectations, Culture, and Clout: The Dynamics of Diversity in Work Groups." In *Diversity in Work Teams: Research Paradigms for a Changing Workplace,* eds. S. E. Jackson and M. N. Ruderman. Washington, D.C. http://dx.doi.org/10.1037/10189-001

McKeegan, D., and C. McKeegan. March 18, 2015. "5 Must-Ask Questions When Recruiting A Virtual Team." *Entrepreneur.* https://www.entrepreneur.com/article/244025

Meirhoefer, A. February 24, 2008. "Trust = Credibility, Reliability and Intimacy, Divided by Self-Interest." http://thesop.org/story/training/2008/02/24/trust-credibilityreliability-and-intimacy-divided-by-self-interest.php

Meyerson, D., F. E. Weick, and R. M. Kramer. 1996. "Swift Trust and Temporary Groups." In *Trust in Organizations: Frontiers of Theory and Research*, eds. R. Kramer and T. Tyler. Thousand Oaks, CA: Sage Publications, pp. 166–95. http://dx.doi.org/10.4135/9781452243610.n9

Mochal, T. November 12, 2007. "10 Tips for Managing Virtual Teams." *techrepublic.com.* https://www.techrepublic.com/blog/10-things/10-tips-for-managing-virtual-teams

Montoya-Weiss, M., A. P. Massay, and M. Song. November, 2017. "Getting it Together: Temporal Coordination and Conflict Management in Global Virtual Teams." *Academy of Management Journal* 44, no. 6. https://doi.org/10.5465/3069399

Morrison, E. W., and S. L. Robinson. January, 1997. "When Employees Feel Betrayed: A Model of How Psychological Contract Violation Develops." *Academy of Management Review* 22, no. 1, pp. 226–56. https://doi.org/10.5465/amr.1997.9707180265

Muli-Kituku, V. 2006. "Top 7 Tips on How to Benefit from Symbiotic Workplace/Business Relationships." *kituku.com.* http://www.kituku.com/article_template.php?id=103

Nemiro, J. n.d. "Wieck's Seven Properties of Sense Making and Related Challenges for Virtual Teams." *Human Capital Review.* http://www.humancapitalreview.org/content/default.asp?Article_ID=558, (Accessed September 10, 2018).

Ngo-Mai, S., and A. Raybaut. May 10, 2007. "Swift Trust and Virtual Team Dynamics." *Universite de Nice-Sophia Antipolis.* https://www.academia.edu/15325315/Swift_trust_and_virtual_ team_dynamics

Northouse, P. G. 2013. *Leadership: Theory and Practice,* 6th ed. Thousand Oaks, CA: Sage Publications.

Nunes, S. T., G. S. Osho, and C. Nealy. December, 2004. "The Impact of Human Interaction on the Development of Virtual Teams." *Journal of Business & Economics Research* 2, no. 12. https://doi.org/10.19030/ jber.v2i12.2953

Panteli, N., and R. Tucker. December, 2009. "Power and Trust in Global Virtual Teams." *Communications of the ACM,* 52, no. 12, pp. 113–5, https://dl.acm.org/citation.cfm?id=1610282

Payton, S. May, 2010. *So Far, So Good? Many Managers Run Teams Spread across Continents, Cultures and Time Zones. Scott Payton Learns How to Make Such Long-Distance Relationships Work Seamlessly. Financial Management (UK).* The Free Library.

Perri, C. n.d. "10 Things to Hate About Sleep Loss." *WebMD.com.* https://www.webmd.com/sleep-disorders/features/10-results-sleep-loss#1, (Accessed September 12, 2018).

Piccoli, G., and Ives, B. September, 2003. "Trust and the Unintended Effects of Behavior Control in Virtual Teams." *MIS Quarterly* 27, no. 3, pp. 365–95. https://doi.org/10.2307/30036538

Pintrich, P. R., and Schunk, D. H. 2013. *Motivation in Education: Theory, Research and Applications.* London, UK: Pearson.

Pitts, V. E., N. A. Wright, and L. C. Harkabus. 2012. "Communication in Virtual Teams: The Role of Emotional Intelligence." *Journal of Organizational Psychology* 12, no. ¾. http://www.na-businesspress.com/ JOP/PittsVE_Web12_3__4_.pdf

Powell, A., G. Piccoli, and B. Ives. December, 2004. "Virtual Teams: A Review of Current Literature and Directions for Future Research." *The Data base for Advances in Information Systems* 35, no. 1, pp. 6–32. https://doi.org/10.1145/968464.968467

Reynolds, G. October 28, 2015. *Transformational Leadership and Organizational Change.* Penn State Leadership Blog. State College, PA: Penn State University.

Rampton, J. January 14, 2016. "10 Qualities of People with High Emotional Intelligence." *Inc.* https://www.inc.com/john-rampton/10-qualities-of-people-with-high-emotional-intelligence.html

Robey, D., H. M. Khoo, and C. Powers. September, 1999. "Situated Learning in Cross-Functional Virtual Teams." *IEEE Transactions on Professional Communication* 43, no. 1, pp. 51–66, https://doi.org/10.1109/47.826416

Robinson, S. December, 1996. "Trust and Breach of the Psychological Contract." *Administrative Science Quarterly* 41, no. 4, 574–99. https://doi.org/10.2307/2393868

Robinson, S. L., and D. M. Rousseau. May, 1994. "Violating the Psychological Contract: Not the Exception but the Norm." *Journal of Organizational Behavior*, 15, pp. 245–59. http://dx.doi.org/10.1002/job.4030150306

Rousseau, D. M. 2000. *Psychological Contract Inventory Technical Report.* Pittsburgh, PA: Heinz School of Public Policy and Graduate School of Industrial Administration, Carnegie Mellon University.

Rousseau, D. M. 1989. "Psychological and Implicit Contracts in Organizations." *Employee Responsibilities and Rights Journal* 2, pp. 121–139.

Rousseau, D. M. September, 1990. "New-hire Perceptions of their Own and their Employer's Obligations: A Study of Psychological Contracts." *Journal of Organizational Behavior* 11, no. 5, pp. 389–400. https://doi.org/10.1002/job.4030110506

Rousseau, D. M. 1995. *Psychological Contracts in Organizations: Understanding Written and Unwritten Agreements.* Thousand Oaks, CA: Sage Publications.

Sarker, S., and S. Sahay. March 2004. "Implications of Space and Time or Distributed Work: An Interpretive Study of US-Norwegian Systems Development Teams." *European Journal of Information Systems*, 13, no. 1. https://doi.org/10.1057/palgrave.ejis.3000485

Schwartz, J., J. Bersin, and B. Pelster. 2014. *Global Human Capital Trends 2014: Engaging the 21st Century Workforce.* Brazil: Deloitte University Press

Settle-Murphy, N. 2006. "Recognize and Address Early Signs of Virtual Team Dysfunction to Avoid Irrecoverable Problems Later." *IT Today.* http://www.ism-journal.com/ITToday/team_dysfunction.htm

Shpancer, N. December 22, 2010. "Framing: Your Most Important and Least Recognized Daily Ment." *Psychology Today*. https://www.psychologytoday.com/us/blog/insight-therapy/201012/framing-your-most-important-and-least-recognized-daily-ment

Siebdrat, F., M. Hoegl, and H. Ernst. July 1, 2009. "How to Manage Virtual Teams." *MIT Sloan Management Review*.

Smith, W. December 17, 2012. "Leadership—The Psychological Contract at Work." *Coaching Wolf Blog*. http://coachingwolf.com/leadership/leadership-the-psychological-contract-at-work

Snellman, C. L. January 24, 2014. "Virtual Teams: Opportunities and Challenges for e-Leaders." *Procedia—Social and Behavioral Sciences* 110, pp. 1251–61.

Snook, S. A. January 2008. "Love and Fear and the Modern Boss." Special Issue on HBS Centennial. *Harvard Business Review* 86, no. 1.

Spector, P. E. 1997. *Job Satisfaction: Application, Assessment, Cause and Consequences*. London, UK: Sage Publications.

Staples, D. S., and J. Webster. February, 2007. "Exploring Traditional and Virtual Team Members' 'Best Practices.'" *A Social Cognitive Theory Perspective*, pp. 60–97, https://doi.org/10.1177/1046496406296961

Staples, S., and L. Zhao. July, 2006. "The Effects of Cultural Diversity in Virtual Teams versus Face-to-Face Teams." *Group Decision and Negotiation* 15, no. 4, 389–406. https://doi.org/10.1007/s10726-006-9042-x

Storey, J. 2007. *Human Resource Management: A Critical Text*. Boston, MA: Cengage Learning.

Styer, S. October 14, 2010. "Building Trust in Virtual Teams: Real Challenges and Solutions." *The Trust Matters Blog*. http://trustedadvisor.com/trustmatters/building-trust-in-virtual-teams-real-challenges-and-solutions

Nayak, N., and Taylor, J. 2009. "Offshore Outsourcing in Global Design Networks." *ASCE Journal of Management in Engineering* 25, no. 4, pp. 177–84.

The National Institute for Occupational Safety and Health. n.d. "Quality of Work Life Questionnaire." https://www.cdc.gov/niosh/topics/stress/qwlquest.html, (Accessed October 7, 2018).

Thompson, J. A., and J. S. Bunderson. October, 2003. "Violations of Principal: Ideological Currency in the Psychological Contract." *Academy of Management Review* 28, no. 4, pp. 571–82. https://doi.org/10.5465/amr.2003.10899381

Thompson, L. L., E. K. Aranda, S. P. Robbins, and C. Swenson. 2000. *Tools Teams: Building Effective Teams in the Workplace*. London, UK: Pearson.

Tomprou, M., and Nikolaou, I. 2011. "A Model of Psychological Contract Creation upon Organizational Entry." *Career Development International* 16, no. 4, pp. 342–63, http://dx.doi.org/10.1108/13620431111158779

Townsend, A. M., S. M. DeMarie, and A. R. Hendricksen. August 1, 1998. "Virtual Teams and the workplace of the future." *Academy of Management Executives* 12, no. 3. https://doi.org/10.5465/ame.1998.1109047

Turnley, W. H., and D. C. Feldman. December, 1998. "Psychological Contract Violation during Corporate Restructuring." *Human Resource Management* 37, no. 1, pp. 71–83. https://doi.org/10.1002/(SICI)1099-050X(199821)37:1<71::AID-HRM7>3.0.CO;2-S

Turnley, W. H., and D. C. Feldman. July, 1999. "The Impact of Psychological Contract Violations on Exit, Voice, Loyalty, and Neglect." *Human Relations* 52, no. 7, 895–922. https://doi.org/10.1023/A:1016971222029

Van der Vegt, G. S., E. Van de Vliert, and A. Oosterhof. 2003. "Informational Dissimilarity and Organizational Citizenship Behavior: The Role of Intra-Team Interdependence and Team Identification." *Academy of Management Journal* 46, no. 6, pp. 715–27. https://doi.org/10.5465/30040663

Vardi, Y., and E. Weitz. 2004. *Misbehavior in Organizations: Theory, Research, and Management*. Mahwah, NJ: Lawrence Erlbaum Associates.

Virtual Team Builders. n.d. "Boot Camp—Working and Leading Offshore/Onshore Teams." http://virtualteambuilders.com/start-learning/learning/bootcamp/working-and-leading-offshoreonshore-teams, (Accessed October 13, 2018).

Virtual Teams Survey Report. 2016. *The Challenges of Working in Virtual Teams*. New York, NY: RW³ Culture Wizard.

Wadors, P. March 07, 2016. "To Stay Relevant, Your Company and Employees Must Keep Learning." *Harvard Business Review*. https://hbr.org/2016/03/to-stay-relevant-your-company-and-employees-must-keep-learning

Walther, J. B., and J. K. Burgoon. September, 1992. "Relational Communication in Computer Mediated Interaction." *Human Communication Research*. 19, no.1, pp. 14–89.

Watkins, M. June, 2013. "Making Virtual Teams Work: Ten Basic Principles." *Harvard Business Review*. https://hbr.org/2013/06/making-virtual-teams-work-ten

Wellin, M. 2007. *Managing the Psychological Contract: Using the Personal Deal to Increase Business Performance: Using the Personal Deal to Increase Performance*. Abingdon-on-Thames, UK: Routledge.

Welsch, D. E. January, 2003. "Globalisation of Staff Movements: Beyond Cultural Adjustment." *Management International Review* 43, no. 2. pp.149–69.https://www.questia.com/read/1G1-106560973/globalisation-of-staff-movements-beyond-cultural

Witt, D. November 3, 2011. "60% of Work Teams Fail—Top 10 Reasons Why." https://leaderchat.org/2011/11/03/60-of-work-teams-fail%E2%80%94top-10-reasons-why, (Accessed October 14, 2018).

Wolinski, S. n.d. "Leadership Defined." *Free Management Library*. http://managementhelp.org/blogs/leadership/2010/04/06/leadership-defined, (Accessed December 5, 2017).

Woodruffe, C. 1999. *Winning the Talent War: A Strategic Approach to Attracting, Developing and Retaining the Best People*. New York, NY: John Wiley & Sons.

Wool, M. December 21, 2017. "How an Effective Remote Work Culture Can Relieve the Loneliness Epidemic." *Business.com*. https://www.business.com/articles/how-effective-work-culture-can-relieve-loneliness

Woolley, D. R. May 16, 2014. "An independent guide to online collaborative workspaces for virtual teams and e-learning groups." *thinkofit.com*. http://thinkofit.com/webconf/workspaces.htm

Young Entrepreneur Council. February 6, 2018. "10 Traits To Look For When Hiring A Remote Employee." *forbes.com*. https://www.forbes

.com/sites/theyec/2018/02/06/10-traits-to-look-for-when-hiring-a-remote-employee/#15be9b4163df

Yuasa, M., K. Saito, and N. Mukawa. April, 2011. "Brain Activity when Reading Sentences and Emoticons: An fMRI Study of Verbal and Nonverbal Communication." *Electronics and Communications in Japan* 94, no.5, pp. 17–24. https://doi.org/10.1002/ecj.10311

Zofi, Y. 2011. *A Manager's Guide to Virtual Teams.* New York, NY: AMACOM.

About the Authors

Dr. Joseph Brady is a consultant, researcher, and lecturer of marketing and sales management courses at the SBS Swiss Business School in Zurich, Switzerland. His previous written works include chapter contributions about academic case teaching and a peer-reviewed journal article pertaining to student markets in higher education. He is also an experienced sales and marketing professional, with previous roles in both the pharmaceutical and consumer goods industries.

Dr. Garry Prentice is a chartered psychologist with research experience within the marketing, addiction, health, social identity, learning, and quantitative methods areas and is a psychology lecturer at Dublin Business School. His research consultancy work has included constructing questionnaires suitable for assessment of program outcomes, statistical analysis of participant outcomes, and report writing. He has publications within the marketing, addiction, psychology, and social research fields, including conference abstracts, reports, and peer-reviewed journal articles.

Index

Academic theory, 92
Asynchronous communication
    methods, 28

Bad hire, 62
Balanced contract, 52
BEEP-THEM model, 92
    build trust, 92–93
    emotional intelligence, 93–94
    empowerment, 93
    energize team, 97–98
    hire right people, 95–97
    make time to sleep and live,
        98–99
    promises and psychological
        contract, 94
    think multiculturally, 94–95
Breach of contract, 55–57

Centers for Disease Control and
        Prevention (CDC), 68
Coaching, 45, 62, 64, 80
Cognitive incongruence, 56
Commitments. *See* Promises
Communication technology, 1, 7,
        13, 16
    bilateral mode of, 15
Conflicts, 76
Corporate leadership, 57–58
Credibility, and trust, 25
Cultural bias, 72–74, 86
    conflicts, 76
Cultural conundrum, 71–77
Cultural diversity, 26, 73–74, 76

Decision making, 7, 20, 32,
        61–62, 89
Democratic leadership, 9
Digital intelligence (DQ), 13, 14
Direct-to-consumer (DTC)
        advertising, 47, 49

E-leadership, 34
E-mail, 16–17
Emotional intelligence (EI), 41, 77,
        93–94
    defined, 42
    key aspect, 42–43
    organizational training, 44
    and virtual team success, 45
Emotional quotient (EQ), 42, 46, 65
Emotions
    management, 45
    negative, 66
Employee satisfaction, 20, 89
Empowerment, 28, 93
Energize team, 97–98
EQ. *See* Emotional quotient

Face-to-face meetings, 6, 10, 11, 13,
        15, 23, 26, 80
FaceTime, 18, 38
Fear method, 8
Forbes magazine, 43–44
Framing, 72, 75

Geert Hofstede's six dimensions of
        national culture, 74–75
General Social Survey (GSS), 68–69
Global communication technology, 7
GoogleDrive, 16, 17
GoToMeeting, 13, 18
GSS. *See* General Social Survey

Hire right people, 95–97
Hiring for virtual team, 61–64
Honoring commitments, 52–53
Hosted Web Collaboration
        Environments, 17

IBM, 16
Individualism versus collectivism
        (IDV), 74–75

Indulgence versus restraint (IND), 74
Inspiration, 97
Instrumental embeddedness, 27
Internal marketing, 97
Internet, 14, 45
Internet phones, 16–17
Invisible contract, 47–59
Isolation, dark halls of, 79–83

Job satisfaction, 65–69
    attitudinal aspects, 68
    General Social Survey, 68–69
    psychological contract, 88
    "two-factor" theory, 67

Key performance indicators (KPIs),
    19, 20, 41, 48, 97

Leadership, 1–2, 54
    defined, 8
    democratic, 9
    fear method, 8
    love method, 8
    shared, benefits, 28
    symbiosis model, 9–11
Likert-scale survey, 85
Long-term orientation versus short-
    term normative orientation
    (LTO), 74
Love method, 8
LTO. See Long-term orientation
    versus short-term normative
    orientation

Manager
    challenges, 79
    decision making, 8, 20
    meeting times, 34
    skills, 27–28
    team members support, 81
Masculinity versus femininity
    (MAS), 74
Matrix organization, 5
Motivation, 79–83
Multicultural teams, 94–95

National Institute for Occupational
    Safety and Health
    (NIOSH), 68

National Science Foundation, 68
Negative emotions, 66
NIOSH. See National Institute for
    Occupational Safety and
    Health

Organizational culture, 21

Participative leadership. See
    Democratic leadership
PDI. See Power Distance Index
Performance reviews, 37
Polychronic culture, 73
Power Distance Index (PDI), 74
Promises, 50, 55–56, 59, 89, 94
Psychological contract, 8, 48–49, 94
    employee perspective, 50–51, 53
    job satisfaction, 88
    relational, 51–52
    transactional, 51–52
    violation of, 55–56
    in virtual team environment, 57

Qualitative research method, 85
Quality of work life (QWL), 68
Quality over quantity, 27
Quantitative research method, 49, 85
QWL. See Quality of work life

Real-world directors, interviews of,
    87–88
Relational psychological contract,
    51–52
Reliability, and trust, 24–25
Remote employees. See Remote
    workers
Remote workers, 7, 13, 80, 88, 96
Role clarity, 19–20, 88, 97
Role conflict, 20

Schema, 50–51
Senior leaders, interviews of, 87–88
Senior leadership, 66, 85
Senior vice president (SVP), 42
Servant leadership approach, 9
Shared leadership, 28
Situational Leadership Model, 9
Skype, 13, 15, 61, 62
Slack, 13, 16, 17

Social isolation, 80–81
SVP. *See* Senior vice president
Swift trust, 25, 86
Symbiosis model of management,
    9–11

Task interdependence, 80
Team integration, 6
Team management, 6
Team trust, 27
Team web pages, 16–17
Technology, 1–2, 7, 13–21
Teleconferences, 13, 55
Temporal differences, 31–33
Texting, 16–17
Time differences, 31–32, 87
    challenges of, 33
Time to sleep and live, 98–99
Transactional psychological contract,
    51–52
Transformational Leadership Model, 9
Transitional contract, 52
Trust, 86, 88, 92–93
    credibility, 25
    defined, 23
    employee's level of, 56
    reliability and, 24–25
    rocky road to, 23–30
    Swift, 25–26
"Two-factor" theory, 67

Uncertainty avoidance index
    (UAI), 74

Violation, contract, 55–57

Virtual communication, 14
Virtual leaders. *See also* Virtual
    managers
    cultural diversity, 76–77
    promises, 59, 89
Virtual managers, 33–34, 57, 87–89,
    97, 99
Virtual teams (VTs), 1–2, 7
    benefits of, 20, 87
    challenges of, 15, 19, 87
    emotional intelligence, 41–46
    energize people on, 98
    hiring for, 61–62
    management, 7–8
    motivation, 82
    problems in, 80
    psychological contract, 57
    quality over quantity, 27
    role clarity, 19–20
    social network, 81–82
    trust. *See* Trust
Virtual Teams Survey Report, 32
Virtual workspaces, 17
Voice calls, 13
VT managers, key points for,
    29–30
VTs. *See* Virtual teams (VTs)

Work–life balance, 31–32

Year-end review (YER), 37–39, 41,
    47, 65
YER. *See* Year-end review (YER)

Zoom Video, 13

OTHER TITLES IN OUR CORPORATE COMMUNICATION COLLECTION

Debbie DuFrene, Stephen F. Austin State University, *Editor*

- *How to Write Brilliant Business Blogs, Volume I: The Skills and Techniques You Need* by Suzan St. Maur
- *How to Write Brilliant Business Blogs, Volume II: What to Write About* by Suzan St. Maur
- *Public Speaking Kaleidoscope* by Rakesh Godhwani
- *The Presentation Book for Senior Managers: An Essential Step by Step Guide to Structuring and Delivering Effective Speeches* by Jay Surti
- *Managerial Communication and the Brain: Applying Neuroscience to Leadership Practices* by Dirk Remley
- *Communicating to Lead and Motivate* by William C. Sharbrough
- *64 Surefire Strategies for Being Understood When Communicating with Co-Workers* by Walter St. John
- *Business Research Reporting* by Dorinda Clippinger
- *English Business Jargon and Slang: How to Use It and What It Really Means* by Suzan St. Maur
- *Conducting Business Across Borders: Effective Communication in English with Non-Native Speakers* by Adrian Wallwork
- *Strategic Thinking and Writing* by Michael Edmondson
- *Business Report Guides: Research Reports and Business Plans* by Dorinda Clippinger
- *Business Report Guides: Routine and Nonroutine Reports and Policies, Procedures, and Instructions* by Dorinda Clippinger
- *Managerial Communication For Organizational Development* by Reginald L. Bell and Jeanette S. Martin
- *Managerial Communication for Organizational Development* by Reginald L. Bell and Jeanette S. Martin

Announcing the Business Expert Press Digital Library

Concise e-books business students need for classroom and research

This book can also be purchased in an e-book collection by your library as

- *a one-time purchase,*
- *that is owned forever,*
- *allows for simultaneous readers,*
- *has no restrictions on printing, and*
- *can be downloaded as PDFs from within the library community.*

Our digital library collections are a great solution to beat the rising cost of textbooks. E-books can be loaded into their course management systems or onto students' e-book readers. The **Business Expert Press** digital libraries are very affordable, with no obligation to buy in future years. For more information, please visit **www.businessexpertpress.com/librarians**. To set up a trial in the United States, please email **sales@businessexpertpress.com**.